Music Rhapsody

Kids make Music.. Babies make Music Too!

by Lynn Kleiner
with Cecilia Riddell

Editor: **Debbie Cavalier**
Engraving: **Mark Young**
Layout Artist: **Debbie Johns Lipton**
Puppet Illustration: **Joey Klucar**

D1239551

DEDICATION

This book is dedicated to my mom, Lila Valdivia in gratitude for your example, your teaching, and your constant support.

PREFACE

The materials presented in this book are ones that I have enjoyed and found to be very successful with babies, toddlers and young children (parents and teachers, too!). For many years my friend and colleague Cecilia Riddell urged me to write down all my favorites so they could be shared with other teachers. This sounded like an overwhelming project as I am a mother of two young children, running a fast growing music school, and very busy with teacher training and workshops!

When I received the invitation from Debbie Cavalier to have Warner Bros. Publications publish my collection of materials, I immediately knew that I would have the support, assistance and hard work of Cecilia to get the job done.

Though I have used these materials for over 20 years, it was Cecilia Riddell who assisted with songs that had not been notated, wrote down explanations as I dictated, (always on the run to one of the schools) and wrote out directions to make the puppets. Cecilia's strong commitment to this project made it a reality.

ACKNOWLEDGEMENTS

Thank you to all the Music Rhapsody teachers, parents, and students who allowed your classes to be photographed. Thank you Janet Green Reid, Maggie Murray-Lee, and Don Silvas for your photographs.

Thank you to Debbie Cavalier for all your help and support in creating this book.

Special thanks to Samantha Cho, Penelope Scott Greeven, and Joyce Weiss for puppet design. Thanks to Shari Lewis and Alice Olsen.

KIDS MAKE MUSIC,
BABIES MAKE MUSIC TOO!

by **Lynn Kleiner**
with **Cecilia Riddell**

INTRODUCTION
THE EARLY CHILDHOOD MUSIC EXPERIENCE
Making it Successful, Making it Joyful, Making it Musical!

THE TEACHER:
- is animated, energetic and enthusiastic.
- is happy to sit on the floor with the children and participate with them.

THE LESSONS:
- contain games and songs for solo singing (pitch matching).
- include both structured and unstructured movement activities and instrument playing.
- contain active listening lessons, which incorporate movement, instrument playing, props, and other visuals.

4

THE CLASSROOM:

- is a music room, free from toys and other distractions.
- if not a dedicated music room, has been arranged to provide the most possible space and the fewest distractions, with tables and other furniture moved aside.
- has a cabinet where the instruments are contained in baskets on shelves, out of sight until they are needed.
- has space for circle games and other movement activities.

THE INSTRUMENTS:

- are easy to play but are not toys.
- have the best possible tone quality, as well as durability.
- are kept separate from toys, props and other non-musical items.
- are abundant enough so that children can play many of the same small instruments at the same time.
- are introduced in musical and interesting ways (see "The Fire Truck" and "Somebody's Knockin'").

THE PROPS:

- are lively, and chosen because they teach the musical activity quickly and effectively (see the little bag of tools for "The Little Shoemaker").
- are personal and topical, such as your family photos to introduce "On My Trip," or your aquarium guide book for the sea lion and otter song, "Simone and Otto."
- are kept in a special bag or box or other container such as a suitcase, a bucket, or a picnic basket.
- include attractive, colorful, high quality books, flannel board items, and puppets.

THE SONGS:

- are short.
- have a limited range.
- include repetition to aid in-tune singing.
- can be sung easily.
- will very soon be sung by the children without adult accompaniment.
- include solo singing parts and games, but have parts for the group, too (see "Red Hen Song," "Simone and Otto" and "Cock-a-Doodle Doo").

THE TRANSITIONS:

- are musical (they are songs, too).
- focus on starting the class and keeping it going without lapses of time when children can become distracted or disruptive.
- help the teacher collect the instruments or props quickly, efficiently, with everyone helping.
- give directions that the children will learn to sing as they make a circle, sit down, and so on.

THE MUSIC MANNERS:

- teach respect for the music and the instruments.
- teach respect for the children who may be singing alone or playing a special instrumental part.
- enable the teacher to incorporate a very active approach, so that even listening to a recording can be accomplished with movement, props, or small instrumental accompaniments.

ABOUT THE ORFF-SCHULWERK

Carl Orff, German composer and music educator (1895-1982), devised the basic musical texts for the Schulwerk with his associate, Gunild Keetman. These texts are models for teachers worldwide. In the Orff approach, children make music with activities that are natural and enjoyable for them: singing, rhyming, dancing, and playing instruments. The songs in this book have been selected or composed to follow the philosophical and practical aims of the Orff-Schulwerk. They are simple, short songs that relate to a child's world of fantasy and experience. Children can master them without special training. This learning process requires attentive listening, decision-making, concentration, cooperation, and sensitivity to rhythm and tone, singing in tune, and playing with others in musical time. Above all, the songs are meant to be enjoyed.

Orff instruments are pitched percussion instruments that were fashioned by Carl Orff from African, Indonesian, and European models. Orff instruments include xylophones, metallophones, and glockenspiels in a number of voicings. They are bright, magical and energetic and are perfectly suited to accompany, support, and guide young singers. Above all, they invite participation.

There are two terms related to the Orff instruments that are referred to throughout this book: PENTATONIC and BORDUN. These musical terms are defined as follows.

1. **PENTATONIC** refers to a five-tone scale, specifically the 1st, 2nd, 3rd, 5th, and 6th scale tones of the major scale. To help ensure a child's success, tone bars not belonging to a particular pentatonic scale can be removed, as illustrated below.

C PENTATONIC BARS

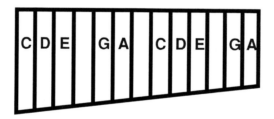

G PENTATONIC BARS

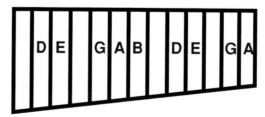

F PENTATONIC BARS

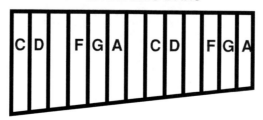

2. **BORDUN** refers to an accompaniment played on the lowest sounding xylophones and metallophones. The bordun consists of the repetition of the 1st and 5th scale tones (also called "DO" and "SO"). A bordun is perfect for accompanying a pentatonic melody. The most common bordun is easy enough for a pre-school age child to play:

BORDUN in C

TEACHING SUGGESTION:

Encourage the children to walk around the Orff instruments (not over them); make sure they use two hands to remove the bars; discuss the best ways to produce beautiful sounds from them with the mallets. Make sure all instruments, large or small, are brought out and put away with great care and respect; the teacher's example will be imitated by the children.

ALL THE LITTLE FIREFIGHTERS

ALL THE LITTLE FIREFIGHTERS,
SLEEPING IN A ROW,
"DING!" GOES THE BELL,
AND DOWN THE POLE THEY GO.

Lie on your back and place baby on your legs (as shown). With your knees bent, bounce your legs gently as you recite the rhyme. On the word "ding" you can imitate the fire bell by rolling your tongue; or another person can ring a triangle. Say the word "down" by sliding your voice from high to low and bring your legs up straight to slide baby "down the pole." Give baby a big hug and kiss and start the game again.

Traditional

APPLE TREE

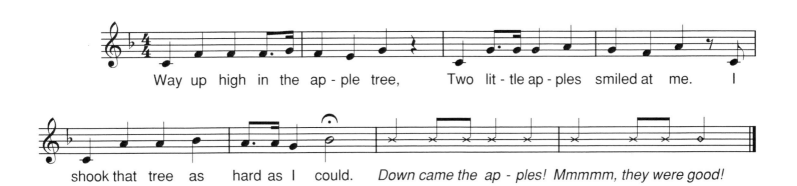

Way up high in the ap - ple tree, Two lit - tle ap - ples smiled at me. I

shook that tree as hard as I could. *Down came the ap - ples! Mmmmm, they were good!*

Lie on your back and place baby on your legs. With your knees bent, bounce your legs gently as you sing the song. On "shook that tree" give baby a gentle jiggle. Pause, and say the word "down" by sliding your voice from high to low. Bring your legs up as you straighten them and slide baby "down the tree." Give baby a big hug and kiss and start the game again.

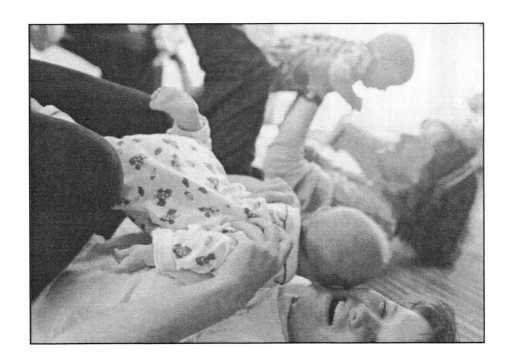

Traditional
Adapted by LYNN KLEINER

A TISKET, A TASKET

A tis - ket, a tas - ket, my lit - tle yel - low bas - ket, and

you can make my lit - tle egg shake if I stop my song be - hind you!

Shake, shake this - a - way, Shake, shake that - a - way, Shake, shake this - a - way, then, oh then.

A Children sing as the teacher, who is "IT," moves around the outside of the circle, carrying a basket with an egg shaker inside. On the word "you," the teacher stops next to a child, who takes the shaker from the basket and goes to center of the circle.

B All sing and imitate the child in the center as he or she moves to "shake, shake." After the B section ends, this child becomes "IT" and the game starts over.

If you have enough shaker eggs for the whole class, it's fun to let the children keep the egg after they've made up their dance for the remainder of the game. This helps everyone see who needs a turn.

LYNN KLEINER

THE BAKERY TRUCK

Discuss with the children the different kinds of baked goods that can be found at a bakery. (Pictures are helpful for children who have trouble thinking of answers.) Teacher wears a baker's hat and moves about the room with a hand drum that serves as a steering wheel for the Baker's make-believe truck. The children stand in a scattered formation or in a circle. The Baker stops in front of a child and sings the question, "What do you see?" and shows the child the hand drum, as if it contained something good to eat. The Baker waits for the child's response. The Baker reinforces the child's response by repeating it (see above). A second bakery item is added by the solo singer, who then becomes the Baker.

THE BAKERY TRUCK

VARIATION 1:

After taking a turn, the solo singer can play a percussion instrument, keeping the beat or repeating a rhythm pattern (an ostinato). Ostinato patterns can accumulate as the singing game progresses.

VARIATION 2:

Teacher can introduce contrasting small percussion instruments to play on the steady beat OR on the quiet beats (rests). After the solo singing, the teacher recites:

PLAY-ING ON THE HAND DRUM, THAT'S YOUR TREAT!   YOU CAN PLAY THE STEA-DY BEAT!

or

HERE IS THE TRI - AN-GLE, THAT'S YOUR TREAT!   YOU CAN PLAY ON   QUI - ET BEATS!

THE BAKERY TRUCK

VARIATION 3:

Introduce the following instrumental accompaniments:

BORDUN

Teacher recites these words, keeping the beat with patschen
(a term which means to keep a steady beat on one's lap).

BIG C, BIG G, THAT'S YOUR TREAT! YOU CAN PLAY THE STEA-DY BEAT.

SOUND CLUSTERS

Teacher recites these words, indicating when to play on rests with a clap on each rest. The instruments are prepared in C pentatonic. The children select two pitches to play from the tone cluster.

A-NY PEN-TA-TON-IC NOTES, THAT'S YOUR TREAT! YOU CAN PLAY ON QUI-ET BEATS!

C Pentatonic tone cluster

Traditional
Arranged by LYNN KLEINER

BAYUSHKA BAYU

1. Go to sleep my dar - ling ba - by, Ba - yush - ka, Ba - yu.
2. I will tell you ma - ny sto - ries, if you close your eyes.

See, the moon is shin - ing on you, Ba - yush - ka, Ba - yu.
Go to sleep my dar - ling ba - by Ba - yush - ka, Ba - yu.

*This chord progression can be simplified. Substitute D chord for F; g minor for Eb, and D for c minor in these two measures.

BABY, TODDLER:

Gently rock baby or toddler while singing this lullaby.

PRE, K- PRI:

Invite children to play the chimes, finger cymbals, and triangles. Ask when they think their instrument would add a beautiful sound to the song. Teacher can tell the children to play gently and softly, in the same manner that they would rock a baby to sleep.

Traditional
Arranged by LYNN KLEINER

THE BEAR WENT OVER THE MOUNTAIN

ALL:

Oh, the bear went ov - er the moun - tain, the bear went ov - er the

moun - tain, the bear went ov - er the moun - tain to see what he could see.

SOLO: LAST TIME ALL:

I see a _____   Oh, the

bear went in - to his cave, ___ the bear went in - to his cave, ___ the

bear went in - to his cave _____ and then he went to sleep.

Children march around the room while singing the song. They pause on "mountain" and draw an upward curve in the air showing the shape of the two-note melody (G - B). On the next words, "to see," they shade their eyes.

During the solo section the teacher holds a pretend microphone in front of the soloist who sings, "I see a lake," etc. The solo section can be repeated by several different children in a row so that more solo singing can be heard. Show a picture of a mountain scene or a forest to help very young solo singers think of words to sing.

Encourage children to make up additional verses. Answers may include: The bear went "through the forest," "over the bridge," "over the river," "to the mall," and so on.

BELL HORSES

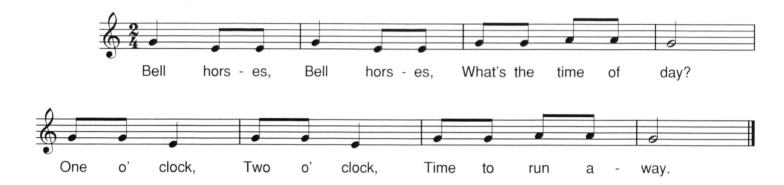

Bell hors - es, Bell hors - es, What's the time of day?

One o' clock, Two o' clock, Time to run a - way.

MISTRESS MARY, QUITE CONTRARY.
HOW DOES YOUR GARDEN GROW?
WITH SILVER BELLS AND COCKLE SHELLS,
AND PRETTY MAIDS ALL IN A ROW.

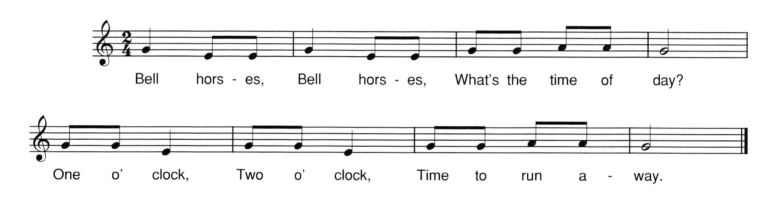

Bell hors - es, Bell hors - es, What's the time of day?

One o' clock, Two o' clock, Time to run a - way.

ONE, TWO, THREE, FOUR.
JINGLE AT THE KITCHEN DOOR.
FIVE, SIX, SEVEN, EIGHT.
JINGLE AT THE GARDEN GATE.

Bell hors - es, Bell hors - es, What's the time of day?

One o' clock, Two o' clock, Time to run a - way.

BELL HORSES

"Bell Horses" is enjoyed as a chair game. Adults bounce babies on their lap to the beat, then pause to say, "Run Little Horse!" Pause again and begin bouncing very fast. The toddler can run around the room at the end of the song, until the teacher or leader says, "Find your horses!" Toddlers climb back on adults' laps and repeat the song.

PRE, K-PRI:

"Bell Horses" can become a movement game. Lining up on one side of the room, children play jingle bells and bounce knees to the beat while singing the song. After singing "time to run away," the children run to the other side of the room, where they speak one of the poems while keeping a steady beat.

A simple bordun on the low xylophones and/or metallophones can accompany "Bell Horses."

Other xylophones and metallophones prepared in C pentatonic can keep the beat, improvising their part by choosing any of the pentatonic pitches shown below.

C PENTATONIC BARS

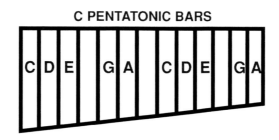

While the children speak "Mistress Mary," the metallophones and glockenspiels are most appropriate to accompany the poem with their bright sounds. For "One, Two, Three, Four," xylophones can play on the numbers (the quarter notes). Glockenspiels can play eighth notes on lines 2 and 4 of the rhyme.

Add temple blocks to create the sound of trotting horses during "Bell Horses."
Add hanging chimes and other metal sounds (triangles, finger cymbals) during
"Mistress Mary." Add contrasting wood percussion, such as rhythm sticks or claves
on the numbers "One, Two, Three, Four." Add jingle bells on lines 2 and 4 of this rhyme.

BIG BEAR

Big   bear,   big   bear,   what   do   you   see?

Hand drum plays half note values; voices are low; tempo is slow.

I   see   a   rab - bit,   hop - ping   by   me.

Rab - bit, rab - bit,   what do you   see?   I   see a   lit - tle mouse   run-ning by   me.

Hand drum now keeps quarter note values; voices are in middle range.

Lit - tle mouse, lit - tle mouse, what do you   see?   I   see a hole in the ground, can't catch me!

Hand drum now keeps eighth notes; voices are faster and high pitched.

After the word "me!" players quickly move hands behind their backs, emphasizing the final beat (a rest).

PRE:

All keep the beat on hand drums while reciting verses about the bear, the rabbit, and the mouse as described above.

K-PRI:

When the children have mastered drumming the rhythm of the rhyme, perform the rhythm without speaking; use "inner-hearing."

Traditional
Arranged by LYNN KLEINER

B-I-N-G-O

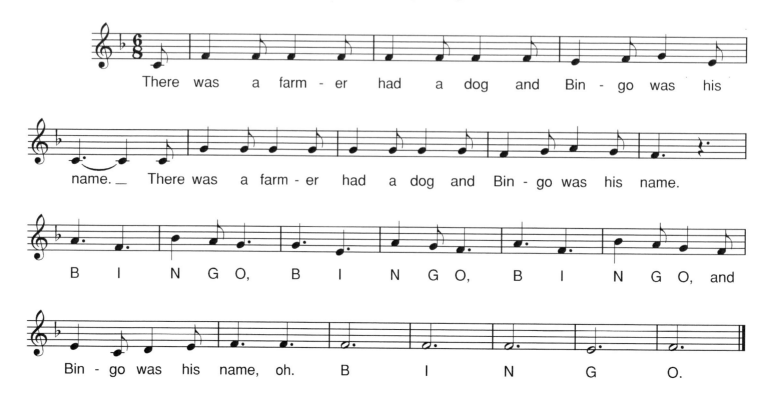

There was a farm-er had a dog and Bin-go was his

name. __ There was a farm-er had a dog and Bin-go was his name.

B I N G O, B I N G O, B I N G O, and

Bin-go was his name, oh. B I N G O.

BABY, TODDLER:

A parent with a baby at home can walk around a room holding the baby outward during the first half of the song. On the slow-spelling part of "B - I - N - G -" walk closer and closer to a mirror. Retreat from the mirror on the final "O."

A group of parents with babies and toddlers carry their children facing outward as they perform the dance.

B-I-N-G-O

PRE, K-PRI:

Children form a circle with the teacher. Walk to the right (or to the left) to the beat while singing the first half of the song. Face the center and take little steps forward — one for each elongated letter, "B - I - N - G -." On "O" everyone shuffles backward to reform the original circle. The game starts again.

Teacher can change the lyrics from the dog's name, BINGO, to a child's name.
For example:

"There was a boy, a little boy, and Lucas was his name. L- U- C-A- S . . . "

Names with more or fewer than five letters can be adapted into the rhythm of the song.
For example:

Three letters:

B E N____

Four letters:

M A R K

Six letters:

M A R T H A

Seven letters:

L A V O N N E

Eight letters:

J E N N I F E R

Traditional
Music by LYNN KLEINER

COCK-A-DOODLE DOO!

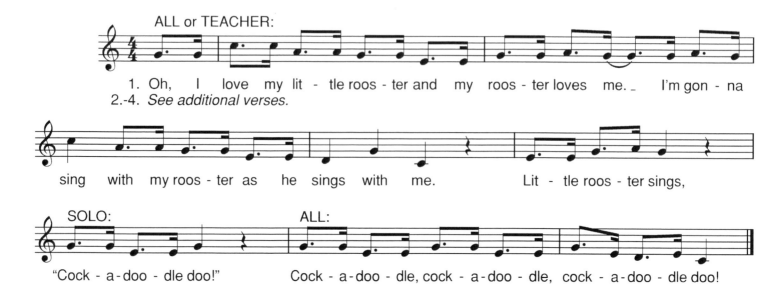

ALL or TEACHER:

1. Oh, I love my lit - tle roos - ter and my roos - ter loves me. _ I'm gon - na
2.-4. *See additional verses.*

sing with my roos - ter as he sings with me. Lit - tle roos - ter sings,

SOLO: **ALL:**

"Cock - a - doo - dle doo!"   Cock - a - doo - dle, cock - a - doo - dle, cock - a - doo - dle doo!

2. Oh, I love my little piggy and my piggy loves me.
   I'm gonna sing with my piggy as he sings with me.
   Little piggy sings,
       SOLO: Oink, oink, oink!
   Little rooster sings,
       SOLO: Cock-a-doo-dle doo,
       ALL: Cock-a-doo-dle, cock-a-doo-dle, cock-a-doo-dle, doo!

3. Oh, I love my little horsey . . . Little horsey sings,
       SOLO: Neigh, neigh, neigh!
   Little piggy sings,
       SOLO: Oink, oink, oink.
   Little rooster sings,
       SOLO: Cock-a-doodle-doo.
         ALL: Cock-a-doo-dle, cock-a-doo-dle, cock-a-doo-dle, doo!

4. Oh, I love my little lamb . . . Little lamb sings . . . Little horsey
   sings. . . Little piggy sings . . . Little rooster sings . . .

As shown above, the teacher cues each animal solo as the solos accumulate.

Stick puppets or finger puppets can be used by the solo singers. Other children can play maracas or shaker eggs as they sing the "cock-a-doodle-cock-a-doodle, cock-a-doodle-doo," which ends each verse.

Puppet-making instructions begin on page 100.

THE COLORS ARE GLIDING

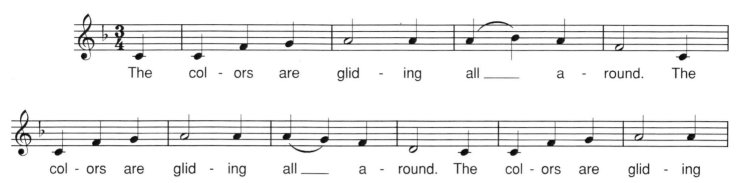

The col - ors are glid - ing all ___ a - round. The

col - ors are glid - ing all ___ a - round. The col - ors are glid - ing

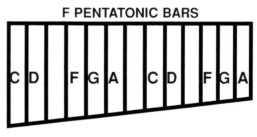

all ___ a - round, and now all our col - ors will fall to the ground.

Now we'll take our colors and lay them out flat.
Then fold them all neatly like this and like that.
Then fold them all neatly like this and like that,
And go to the basket and put them all back.

Movement with different colored scarves is meant to accompany this song. Have the children follow the lyrics as a guide to playing with the scarves.

For a simple and beautiful accompaniment, metallophones set up in F pentatonic, can be played once on each measure. Children with two or four mallets can strike pentatonic bars, changing at random on the first beat of every measure.

F PENTATONIC BARS

C D F G A C D F G A

See other creative movement and scarf songs in this publication including "Colors Around Us," "Merry-Go-Round," and "Stormy Day."

Lyrics by SUSAN CAMBIQUE TRACEY
Melody by MARIA KOUBESERIAN

COLORS AROUND US

Col - ors   a - round us.   col - ors   sur-round   us.   Col - ors,   col - ors,

TEACHER: SOLO:

make our   world bright.   What   col - or   does   Bil - ly   have?   Blue. ___

PRE:

Movement with scarves is a perfect activity for "Colors Around Us." Teacher holds a pretend microphone in front of the soloist, inserting the child's name. For variation, the teacher can hold up a scarf, singing "What color is this?" Singing the name of the color reinforces both vocabulary and tone matching.

K-PRI:

The teacher's question can elicit a longer answer or even a conversation.

"Colors Around Us" works well in rondo form. After moving with scarves during the A section (song), children can add their own speech such as "Blue is the ocean" or "The sun is yellow" and improvise to follow their words. These improvisations become the B, C, D, and E sections.

Easy and beautiful elaborations on Orff barred instruments can be made with this song. With instruments prepared in F pentatonic, children can play on the beats where the word "colors" is sounded. They may choose any bar or bars, playing with one or two mallets. At the end, these children can play once on the final beat, marking the rest following the word "bright." Metal sounds are particularly appropriate.

F PENTATONIC BARS

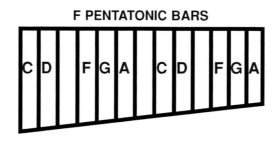

See related songs with scarves: "Merry-Go-Round," "Stormy Day," and "The Colors Are Gliding."

COME AND PLAY THE TAMBOURINE

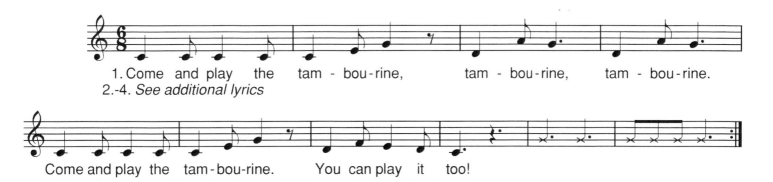

1. Come and play the tam-bou-rine, tam-bou-rine, tam-bou-rine.
2.-4. *See additional lyrics*

Come and play the tam-bou-rine. You can play it too!

2. Two thumbs are playing the tambourine, tambourine, tambourine,
Two thumbs are playing the tambourine. You can play it too!

3. Jingle and shake the tambourine . . . too!

4. Play your own way on the tambourine . . . too!

Have the children sit on the floor with tambourines in front of them. Encourage them to explore different ways to make sounds with the tambourines. Add the song, keeping the tambourines on the floor to accommodate "Two thumbs are playing the tambourine." At "Jingle and shake" children should pick up the instruments and play them. Invite students to create new verses such as "March and play your tambourine," "Play softly on your tambourine," and so on.

Melody by LUDWIG VAN BEETHOVEN
Lyrics by LYNN KLEINER

COME, MY FRIENDS

Come, my friends, and gath - er 'round so we can sing good - bye. ___ We'll

sing and dance an - oth - er day. So long, fare - well good - bye. ___

When children are familiar with this goodbye song, play the classical music from which the tune is derived, the fourth movement of Beethoven's Symphony No. 6. Children enjoy singing "Come, My Friends" with an orchestral accompaniment.

COME TO THE FARM

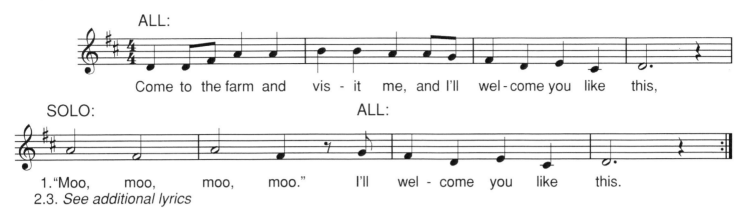

ALL:

Come to the farm and vis - it me, and I'll wel - come you like this,

SOLO:　　　　　　　　　　**ALL:**

1. "Moo, moo, moo, moo." I'll wel - come you like this.
2.3. *See additional lyrics*

2. "Baa, baa, baa, baa." I'll welcome you like this.

3. "Oink, oink, oink, oink." I'll welcome you like this.

"Come to the Farm" is a solo singing song. The teacher can enhance the activity by using felt board cut-outs, finger puppets, or hand puppets of a cow, sheep, pig, and other animals.

PRE:
Use a felt board set-up with a barn. Give animal cut-outs to the children. The children stand up to sing when it's their turn and place the animal on the felt board (any place). Children with a hand or finger puppet, or a stuffed animal, can activate the prop as they sing the solo part.

Puppet-making instructions for "Come to the Farm" are on page 103.

K-PRI:
Older children can learn the song accumulatively; following "Baa, baa," insert the previous solo singer's "Moo, moo," and so on. For a challenge, add more animals to the song.

CRISS CROSS, APPLE SAUCE

POEM	ACTIONS
CRISS CROSS, APPLE SAUCE.	With four long strokes, make two large Xs on baby's back.
SPIDER CRAWLING UP YOUR BACK.	With two fingers, slowly "crawl" up baby's back.
COOL BREEZE!	Gently blow on baby's neck, and pause.
TIGHT SQUEEZE!	Put your arms around baby, hug, and pause.
AND NOW YOU'VE GOT THE SHIVERS!	Tickle all over.

Speak this baby massage rhyme slowly, deliberately, and musically. Keep the beat with your motions and with your voice.

After the baby is familiar with this massage rhyme, you can create extra suspense and anticipation by repeating the motions and the words of the first line before finishing the rhyme. This also extends the steady-beat experience on baby's back.

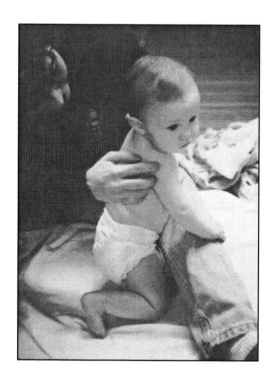

CRISS CROSS

TIGHT SQUEEZE

EXERCISE TO THE BEAT

The music for this activity is on the <u>Kids Make Music, Babies Make Music Too!</u> CD or you can perform the following beat-keeping motions to the steady beat of a favorite recording while baby is lying on his back. Do each motion several times before going on to the next.

MOTIONS:

1. Gently holding baby's wrists, move them to the beat in a bouncing motion: up, up, down, down (repeat), or out, out, in, in (repeat).

2. Gently move one wrist and the opposite ankle to the beat, diagonally, toward each other and away. Tap ankle to wrist on the beat. Switch to baby's other wrist and other ankle. Repeat many times.

3. Hold both ankles and tap feet together, keeping the beat.

4. Hold both ankles and move in parallel motion, bending and straightening baby's knees.

5. Hold both ankles and move in a bicycling pattern.

Babies will let you know which of the movement routines they like best.

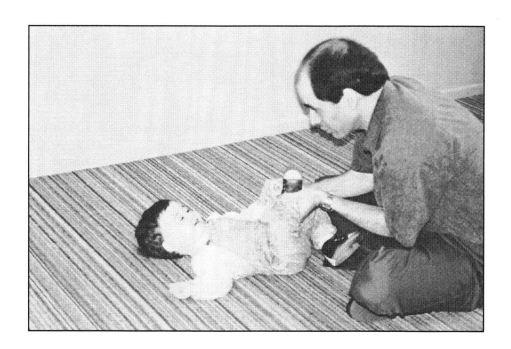

Lyrics by LUCILLE WOOD

THE FIRE TRUCK

1. Hur - ry hur - ry, drive the fire truck, hur - ry hur - ry, drive the fire truck,
2.-6. *See additional lyrics*

hur - ry hur - ry, drive the fire truck, ding, ding, ding, ding, ding!

2. Hurry, hurry, turn the corner. Hurry, hurry, turn the corner.
   Hurry, hurry, turn the corner. Ding, ding, ding, ding, ding!

3. Hurry, hurry, find the fire . . .

4. Hurry, hurry, climb the ladder . . .

5. Hurry, hurry, squirt the water . . .

6. Let's go rest back at the station . . .

With this action song the children pretend to do what each verse suggests. Dramatize the actions!
Pretend to turn the steering wheel, find the fire, turn the corner, climb the ladder, and squirt the water.
At the end, slow down the singing, stretch, yawn, and lie down on the floor. It is also fun to feature
triangles, which play five times with the "Ding, ding, ding, ding, ding!"

TODDLER:

With younger toddlers, parents hide the triangles and bring them out just in time for the little ones to
use their strikers to play. For older toddlers, a teacher holding one triangle can position the instrument in front of a child who is holding a striker; that child plays on cue, and the teacher moves to
another child. Prepared this way, children will understand when to play and will be more successful
when they have their own triangles and strikers.

PRE, K-PRI:

The children can play the pitches So, Fa, Mi, Re, Do on the barred percussion instruments at the end
of each verse. In the key of F they will play the notes C Bb A G F.

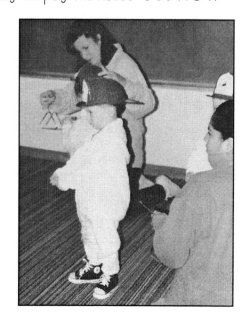

FISH POLE

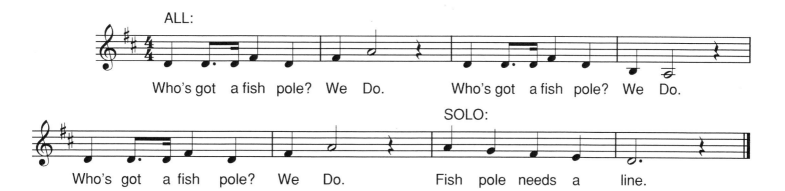

ALL:

Who's got a fish pole? We Do. Who's got a fish pole? We Do.

SOLO:

Who's got a fish pole? We Do. Fish pole needs a line.

K-PRI:

Teacher can cue a solo singer with a pretend microphone. After singing alone, the soloist is rewarded with a piece of chalk or a marker and draws the answer he just sang on the board. What does the fish pole need next? A line, a sun, a boat, a worm, a fish, a hook? Encourage children to draw quickly. The teacher can impose a 30 second drawing-time limit to keep things moving along, if necessary.

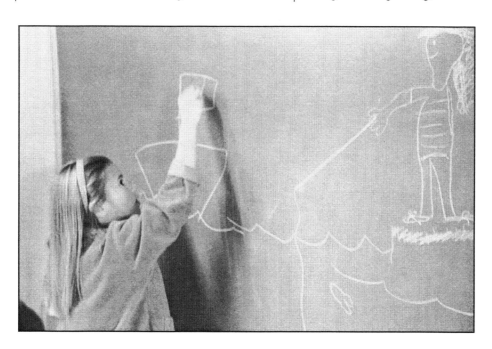

FIVE LITTLE KITTENS

POEM

FIVE LITTLE KITTENS ALL BLACK AND WHITE,

SLEEPING SOUNDLY THROUGH THE NIGHT.

MEOW! MEOW!   MEOW!   MEOW!

MEEEEOOOOW!

TIME TO GET UP NOW!

ACTIONS

Make long, downward strokes from baby's shoulder and off the hand as you speak these two lines.

Hold one of baby's hands. At each of the five "meows," gently massage one finger of baby's hand upward. Start with baby's thumb and end with the little finger.

Run your fingers up the arm, and tickle under the arm to finish.

Repeat, stroking the other arm.

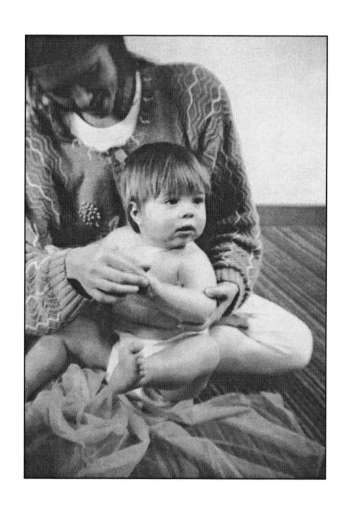

FIVE LITTLE TRIANGLES

FIVE LITTLE TRIANGLES, HANGING IN A ROW.

THE FIRST ONE SAID, "RING ME SLOW."

THE SECOND ONE SAID, "RING ME FAST!"

THE THIRD ONE SAID, "RING ONLY ONCE,
AND LISTEN HOW LONG IT WILL LAST."

THE FOURTH ONE SAID, "I'M LIKE A CHIME!"

THE FIFTH ONE SAID, "IT'S MUSIC TIME!"

Teacher should model the five triangle techniques before asking the children to play the solo parts.

TODDLER:
Parents can hold the triangle or the teacher can bring the triangle to the child. The child holds the striker. Teacher moves from one child to the next for each line of the poem.

PRE, K-PRI:
Each child holds and performs with his own complete instrument.
On "chime," encourage the child to mimic a clock's chime.
The final line, "music time!" (or "recess time," or "dinner time")
suggests rapid strikes, played from within the triangle shape.

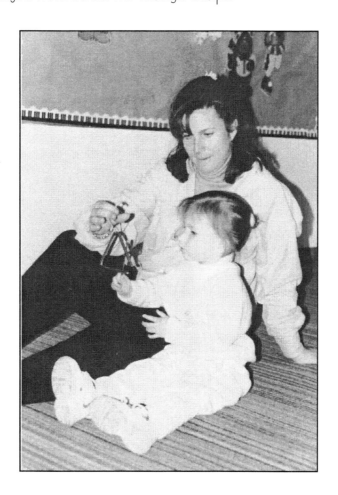

FOLK DANCE

The recording of this dance is on the CD, <u>Kids Make Music, Babies Make Music Too!</u> and is shown in the video, <u>Babies Make Music</u>.

The melody appears below, pitched for recorder, flute or violin solo. The addition of chords will enable a piano or guitar accompaniment. Other folk dance music, in which phrases are grouped into units of eight counts, may be substituted.

FOLK DANCE

Hold baby facing outward and follow the dance steps as shown in the music.

A Section:
Walk forward in a circle formation, moving counterclockwise.

B Section:
Face center of circle and walk in and out to the beat of the music. Turn around once in place for eight counts.

* Raise baby or toddler as you advance forward here; lower him as you walk backward.

GOIN' ON A BIKE RIDE

Go - in' on a bike ride, go - in' on a bike ride,

go - in' on a bike ride, who do you see? Grand-ma's on a bike ride,

Grand-ma's on a bike ride, Grand-ma's on a bike ride, rid - ing with me!

BABY:

As a floor game for babies, parents make up the names of the bike riders and move infant's legs as if riding a bicycle.

TODDLER:

One child walks in a circle with a parent or another adult. At the question, "Who do you see?" some-one's name is sung, and the new child and parent follow. The game continues. One new child and parent are added until the whole class is on the bike ride.

PRE:

For older children this song can be performed in a circle as a solo singing game. A leader walks around the outside of the circle, shoulders and arms moving rhythmically as if steering the bike rhythmically to the right, to the left. On the words, "Who do you see?" the soloist sings the name of a child he has selected to follow him. Two bicycle riders resume the game, then collect a third person, and so on.

GOING ON A PICNIC

Go-ing on a pic-nic, leav-ing right a-way; if it does-n't rain we'll stay all day.

TEACHER: SOLO: ALL:

1. Did you bring the hot dogs? Yes, I brought the hot dogs! Read-y for a pic-nic? Here we go!
2. Did you bring the sal-ad? Yes, I brought the sal-ad!

Solo singers answer the teacher's questions, while everyone sings the rest of "Going on a Picnic."
Props such as a pretend microphone and a picnic basket (with selected objects inside) can be used to
good effect here. Older children enjoy making up the questions for the teacher and/or the group to sing
in response.

A simple bordun can accompany the **A** section of "Going on a Picnic."

GOODBYE SONG

We'll sing good-bye, our time is done. We'll sing good-bye, now ev-'ry-one. We'll sing good-bye, this song will tell, "You make mu-sic ve-ry well."

Every class should end with a special goodbye song such as this or "Come, My Friends." Sung quietly, with a guitar providing a soft accompaniment, a goodbye song brings the class together, giving you an opportunity to affirm with warm appreciation each child's effort and accomplishment. "Closure" is further emphasized when you shake hands and sing "Goodbye _____," to each child.

GRAY SQUIRREL

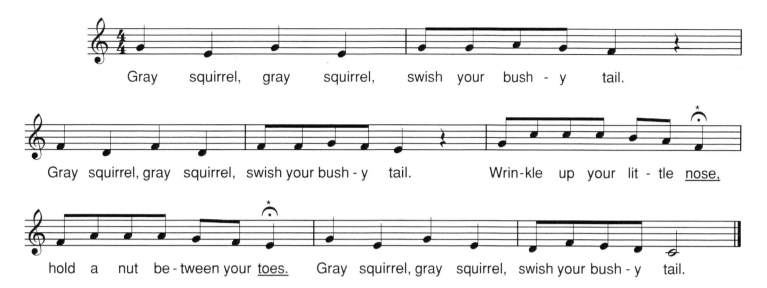

Gray squirrel, gray squirrel, swish your bush - y tail.

Gray squirrel, gray squirrel, swish your bush - y tail. Wrin-kle up your lit - tle nose,

hold a nut be - tween your toes. Gray squirrel, gray squirrel, swish your bush - y tail.

BABY:

Baby lies on back. Parent should position the maraca (shaker) so that baby is holding it too, between parents' hands. Keep the beat as you sing; move baby and maraca from side to side. On the phrase, "wrinkle up your little nose" touch baby's nose. On the next phrase, gently tap baby's ankles together.

TODDLER, PRE:

Toddlers can hold a maraca and move it from side to during the first four measures. Next they will touch the maraca to their noses* and toes,* following the lyrics. Some toddlers will provide the missing words, "nose," and "toes," if you stop and wait for them to sing.

HELLO (ECHO) SONG

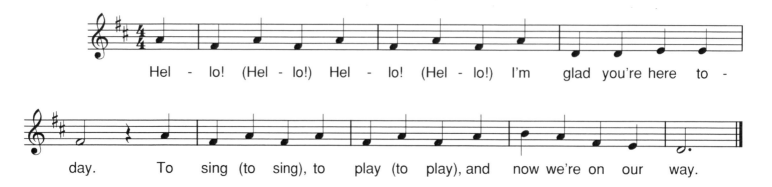

Hel - lo! (Hel - lo!) Hel - lo! (Hel - lo!) I'm glad you're here to -

day. To sing (to sing), to play (to play), and now we're on our way.

"Hello (Echo) Song" is a beginning solo singing song. It is loved by the youngest singers, especially when the teacher uses a finger puppet. The song is sung the first time with the finger puppet who supplies the echo part. Next, the teacher moves near a solo singer with the puppet, and the two of them sing the song. Moving to a different child for each of the SO-MI echo patterns allows for more solo singing opportunities. Play again with all children wearing a finger puppet.*

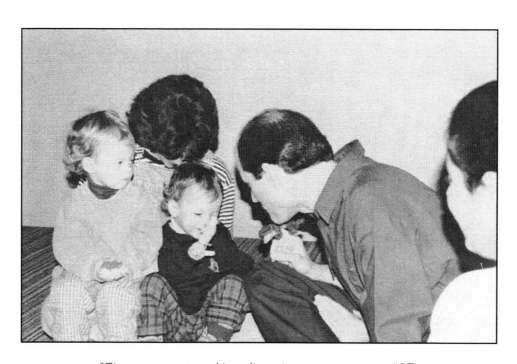

*Finger puppet-making directions are on page 103.

HUMPTY DUMPTY

Parent sits on the floor with baby perched on top of bent knees.
Bounce baby to the beat by lifting toes.

POEM

ACTIONS

HUMPTY DUMPTY SAT ON A WALL.

Bouncing.

HUMPTY DUMPTY HAD A GREAT FALL.

Add a vocal sound effect here; a long, descending "Oooooo."
At the same time, straighten your legs so that baby "falls," but remains upright on your knees.

ALL THE KING'S HORSES AND ALL THE KING'S MEN

Recite the remaining lines with legs straight, but keep little bounces in your knees.

COULDN'T PUT HUMPTY TOGETHER AGAIN.

Now make a vocal glissando upward on "Oooooo" while moving back up to starting position. Pause, and repeat.

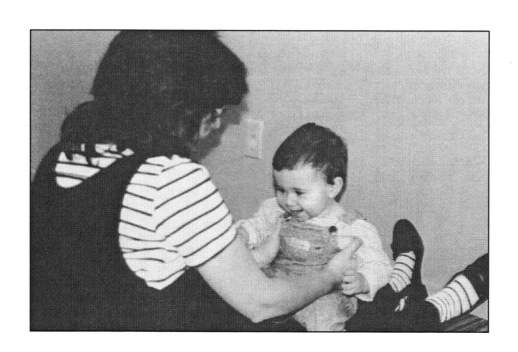

Traditional
Arranged by LYNN KLEINER

I KNOW A LITTLE PONY

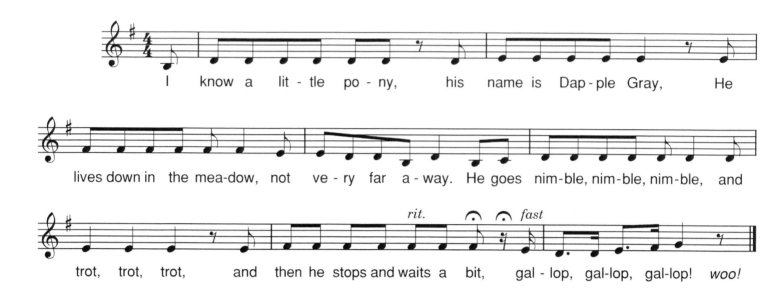

I know a lit-tle po-ny, his name is Dap-ple Gray, He lives down in the mea-dow, not ve-ry far a-way. He goes nim-ble, nim-ble, nim-ble, and trot, trot, trot, and then he stops and waits a bit, gal-lop, gal-lop, gal-lop! *woo!*

Bounce to the beat. Double the bounce motion on "Nimble, nimble, nimble." Return to the beat for "Trot, trot, trot," bouncing a little higher on these three words. PAUSE, then lean forward and sing the song right into the child's ear. Remain still until "Gallop, gallop, gallop." On these words, give baby or toddler three strong bounces. End by lifting child in the air.

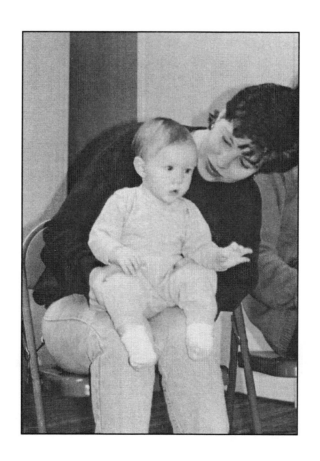

JACK IN THE BOX

Jack in the Box, so qui-et and still.   Will you come out?   Of course I will!

Young singers enjoy pretending to be inside a box. The children can practice popping up on cue to sing, "Of course I will!" After rehearsing this action with everyone, the teacher asks for a volunteer to crouch down inside a large cardboard box. A big plastic bucket or storage container also works well. One child is inside; others move in a circle around the box, singing and keeping the beat. After the word "still" everyone stops and sings, "Will you come out?" The solo singer jumps up with the reply, arms high.

A simple bordun can accompany this song, keeping the beat but stopping at the words "Will you come out?"

Traditional
Arranged by LYNN KLEINER

JIG JOG

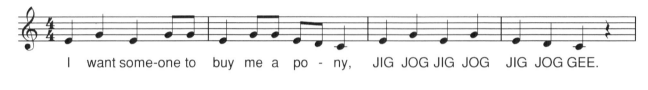

I want some-one to buy me a po - ny, JIG JOG JIG JOG JIG JOG GEE.

Not too fat and not too bo - ny, JIG JOG JIG JOG JIG JOG GEE.

For I want to go for a ride, all a - cross the coun - try - side with a

JIG JOG JIG JOG JIG JOG JIG JOG JIG JOG JIG JOG GEE.

BABY, TODDLER:

"Jig Jog" is enjoyed by babies as a lap game. Sitting on parent's knees, baby faces other children (if there is a class) or faces parent (if at home). Parent sways baby right and left, keeping the beat on the first phrases. On the "jig jogs" bounce the babies gently up and down.

PRE, K-PRI:

On the first phrase, hold rhythm sticks vertically and keep the beat on the legs. Tap the sticks together on the "jig jogs."

Playing Orff instruments, children can improvise on the "jig jog" lyrics.

C PENTATONIC BARS

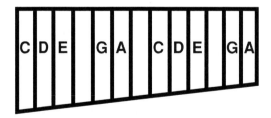

I WANT SOMEONE TO BUY ME A PONY

JIG JOG

LEG OVER LEG

LEG OVER LEG, AS THE

DOG WENT TO DOVER, WHEN HE

CAME TO A STILE . . . (Pause here)

JUMP, HE WENT OVER!

This baby lap game is played with the parent sitting on a chair and the baby facing parent (or facing away, if there are other babies and parents to watch). Keep the beat, bouncing legs until "stile." Pause after the word "stile" to heighten the anticipation of a jump. Bounce and lift baby on "jump," and finish with the words, "he went over!" Give baby a hug and start again.

LITTLE CLOWN

We know you're hid-ing in there! We know you're crouch-ing down! We real-ly want to see you! Come out! Lit-tle clown.

TODDLER:

Pair this song with a pop-up clown puppet or doll.* When child sings "Come out," reward the singer by making the clown appear. Repeat the song many times so that several children have the opportunity to sing this little solo of G to C' (SO to high DO). Each time, start the song with the clown puppet hiding from view. All the children should sing with the teacher on the last lyrics, "little clown."

PRE:

A simple bordun provides a nice accompaniment for this song.

If you have the large C contra-bass bar, this is appropriate to play, also.

The remaining barred instruments (with all bars left on them) can play an ascending glissando (a rapid sound made by drawing the mallet over the bars of the instrument) whenever the clown pops up.

K-PRI:

Children also love to improvise music while the clown dances. Set up the xylophones and metallophones in C pentatonic for this.

C PENTATONIC BARS

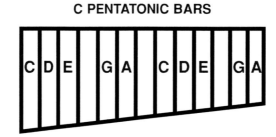

When the clown pops back down into his hiding place, the music should stop. Ask the children to reflect the clown's movements on their instruments. "Is the clown dancing fast or slow? Is he jumping up and down? Is he rising slowly? Falling?" and so on.

See puppet making instructions on page 100.

Traditional melody
Arranged by LYNN KLEINER

LITTLE HORSES

1. Lit - tle hors - es, lit - tle hors - es, come out of your
2.-4. *See additional lyrics*

barn. The door is wide op - en, the sun - shine is warm.

2. Sing melody on "lai."
3. Little horses, little horses, come back to your barn.
   The door is wide open, your blankets are warm.
4. Sing melody on "lai."

MOVEMENT ACTIVITIES:

Teacher designates a barn for the pretend horses (the children).
Two children can pretend to be the closed barn door.

Verse 1.   Children pretend they are horses inside the barn, ready to play in the sunshine.
            The "door" is opened for them at the end of verse 1.
Verse 2.   Children run and gallop while the melody is sung on "lai."
Verse 3.   Children come back to the pretend barn.
Verse 4.   Children sing the "lullaby" music as they "sleep" in the barn.

INSTRUMENTS:

Singing this song without the movement, the children can keep the beat by tapping on
the ribbed tone-block.

Verse 1:   Singing only. Keep mallet inside ribbed tone block
            (like the horses inside the barn).
Verse 2:   Take mallet out and keep the beat on the instrument.
Verse 3:   Continue to sing and play, but by the end of the verse,
            return the mallet to the inside of the tone block, holding it against a shoulder.
            Put the instrument down and pick up finger cymbals.
Verse 4:   Sing the melody slowly and softly on "lai," and
            accompany with finger cymbals.

LITTLE SHOEMAKER

1. There's a wee lit-tle man in a wee lit-tle house, lives ov-er the way, you
2. *See additional lyrics*

see. And he sits at the win-dow and he sews all day mak-ing shoes for you and

me. A *tap, tap, tap, tap, tap, tap, tap, tap, tap, tap, tap, tap, tap, tap, tap, a

tap, tap, tap, tap, tap, tap, tap, mak-ing shoes for you and me.

2. He puts the needle in and out, the thread flies to and fro.
   With his tiny tool he makes the holes, hear the hammer's steady blow.

* A tap, tap, tap . . . making shoes for you and me.

+ Finger cymbals play on the first beat of each measure (but don't expect precise playing from the younger children).
* Wood percussion is played on all the TAP words.

INSTRUMENTS:

Teacher holds up each finger cymbal by the fabric strap with thumb and index (pincher) fingers. Pretending that one cymbal is the "shoe," and the other finger cymbal is the "threaded needle," the teacher holds the "shoe" steady while moving the "needle" in a circular motion. The wide circular sewing motion by one hand causes the moving cymbal to ring the stationary cymbal.

The ribbed tone block plays the shoemaker's taps.

Half the class can play finger cymbals, half can play the tone blocks.

Introduce this song with props. Such items as a shoe or a foam shoe insert, a small bag, a large needle and thread, and a small hammer will bring the song to life.

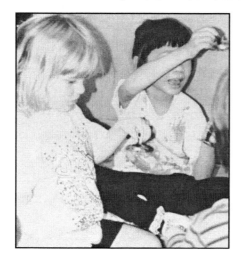

MAGIC TRICK

I can do a ma-gic trick,   If you sing the mag-ic word: Please! __

The teacher walks among the children while singing the song. Children tap the steady beat until the teacher stops in front of someone. The teacher conceals a popsicle stick "rabbit"* inside a black paper cup which serves as a "magician's hat." Showing the magician's hat, the teacher waits until a selected child sings, "Please. . ." At that, the rabbit pops out of the hat. Repeat, selecting different soloists.

A simple bordun can accompany "Magic Trick."

* See instructions for making paper cup and popsicle stick puppets on page 104.

MARCHING

We're march-ing all a - round. We're march-ing all a - round. We're in the band. It's real - ly grand! Oh, what a hap - py sound!

TODDLER:

Marching to the beat of this song helps children gain a good sense of timing. They enjoy choosing an instrument to play as they march. In a classroom, or with a group of children at home, you can appoint leaders to take turns deciding where to march. You can also introduce recorded marching music and discuss the instruments that the orchestra or band members are playing.

PRE, K-PRI:

A simple bordun can accompany this song, keeping the beat on C and G. Use the lowest pitched xylophones and metallophones. Set up the glockenspiels in C pentatonic, too; these higher pitched instruments can then be used to play a tone cluster on each phrase ending, where the rests occur. The child chooses which two pitches to play.

C Pentatonic tone cluster

C PENTATONIC BARS

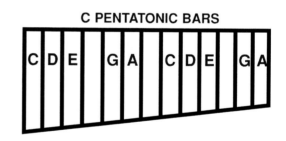

MERRY-GO-ROUND

Round and round the mer - ry - go - round. Mu - sic is

play - ing, a pipe or - gan sound. Up, down, up, down,

gal - lop - ping, gal - lop - ping round and round. Hor - ses and po - nies and

colts and mares, gal - lop - ping, gal - lop - ping round in pairs.

A beautiful activity with this song requires a hula hoop (one for four or five players) and a scarf for each child. Each child holds the hoop with the left hand, and walks counter-clockwise in a circle, a scarf held in the right hand.

LYRICS	ACTIONS
"Round...sound"	Walk
"Up...down"	Stop. Move hoop and scarf up and down.
"Round...sound"	Walk.
"Horses...mares"	Stop. Move hoop and scarf up and down.
"Galloping...pairs"	Walk.

MOTHER AND FATHER AND UNCLE JOHN

MOTHER AND FATHER AND UNCLE JOHN

WENT TO TOWN, ONE BY ONE.

MOTHER FELL OFF . . .

FATHER FELL OFF . . .

BUT UNCLE JOHN WENT ON, AND ON,

AND ON, AND ON, AND ON!

Baby bounces on adult's knees in this chair game. Baby either faces the adult, or if there is a group, baby will enjoy facing outward where he has a view of all the other babies and parents. A moderate up and down bouncing keeps the pulse of the three characters going to "town." Holding infant or toddler securely, adult tilts baby from side to side. Allow him to lean first to one side ("Mother fell off") and then to the other ("Father fell off"). Brought back to an upright position again, baby is bounced longer and gradually faster for the remainder of the rhyme.

Traditional
Arranged by LYNN KLEINER

NAUGHTY KITTY CAT

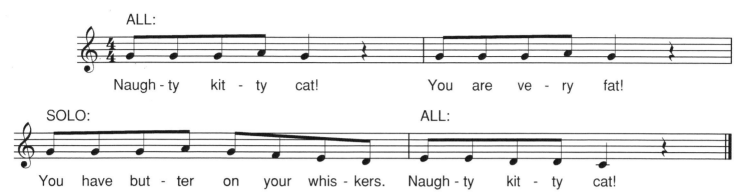

ALL:

Naugh - ty kit - ty cat! You are ve - ry fat!

SOLO: ALL:

You have but - ter on your whis - kers. Naugh - ty kit - ty cat!

Teacher introduces this song with a large fat cat puppet or a stuffed animal. Solo parts are taught next. The cat appears in front of one child, who sings, "You have butter on your whiskers." The group rejoins the song with the final "Naughty kitty cat!" Teacher encourages different singing responses by asking, "What else did he have on his whiskers? Maybe he jumped on your breakfast table," and so on. Answers may include cereal, jam, peanut butter, and so on.

A simple bordun can accompany "Naughty Kitty Cat." Bass xylophone and bass metallophone keep steady beat, as shown.

Children strike bars on glockenspiels (prepared in C pentatonic) where each rest occurs, producing a cluster of pitches.

C Pentatonic tone cluster

C PENTATONIC BARS

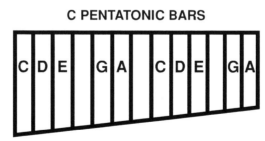

C D E G A C D E G A

THE OLD GRAY CAT

1. The old gray cat is sleep - ing, sleep - ing,
2.-4. *See additional lyrics*

sleep - ing. The old gray cat is sleep - ing in the house.

2. The little mice are creeping, creeping, creeping.
   The little mice are creeping, in the house.
3. The old gray cat is waking . . . in the house.
4. Now everyone is running . . . in the house.

TODDLER:

Beginning by lying down on the floor, children dramatize each verse as it is sung. Children pretend to be the cat. Then they stand up and slowly move like the creeping mouse. Then they lie down again, stretching and waking up like the old cat. On the final verse, children are up again, running.

PRE, K-PRI:

Older children enjoy choosing to be either the cat (in a group) or one of the mice (in a group).

All ages can appreciate the dramatic events in this song. Let each child decide what instruments to play for each verse and how they should be played. For example, the triangle could be played softly for sleeping, the rhythm sticks for creeping, and so on.

A simple pentatonic accompaniment is effective with "The Old Gray Cat." Xylophones and metallophones are set up in G pentatonic as shown, and children improvise the cat's music by selecting pitches to keep the slow beat and tempo on metallophone, while others play the mice music, "creeping" and "running" over the bars of the xylophones on stanzas 2 and 4.

G PENTATONIC BARS

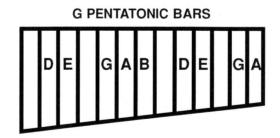

Remember that more than one child can play at each instrument. The two-octave xylophones and metallophones work well if you have large classes.

Traditional
Arranged by LYNN KLEINER

THE OLD WOMAN AND HER PIG

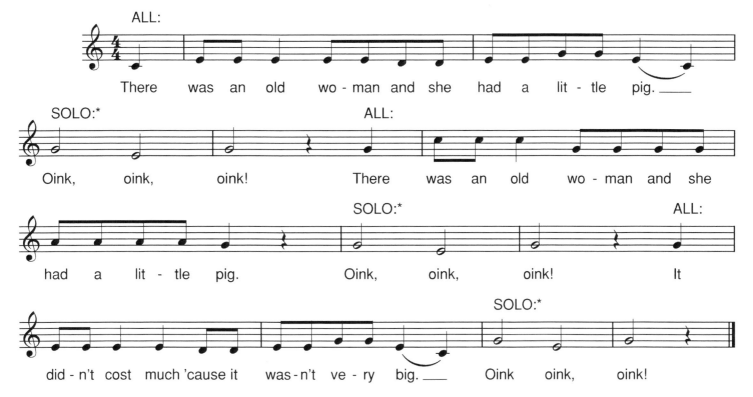

ALL:

There was an old wo - man and she had a lit - tle pig. ___

SOLO:* ALL:

Oink, oink, oink! There was an old wo - man and she

SOLO:* ALL:

had a lit - tle pig. Oink, oink, oink! It

SOLO:*

did - n't cost much 'cause it was - n't ve - ry big. ___ Oink oink, oink!

2. The little old woman kept the pig in the barn. Oink, oink, oink.
   The little old woman kept the pig in the barn. Oink, oink, oink.
   The prettiest thing she had on the farm. Oink, oink, oink.

Pig finger puppet* and "pig" notation are perfect props for this solo singing game. All the children can wear the pig finger puppets. Teacher can vary the little solo tune by asking for the "oinks" to be sung on SO MI SO, or SO SO SO, or (at the end) SO MI DO, as shown on a large drawing of these pitches. The note heads on the staff can be made to resemble pig heads.

*See instructions for finger puppets on page 103.

A simple bordun accompaniment can be added to this song.

ONE LEG, TWO LEGS

ONE LEG, TWO LEGS,

HOT CROSS BUNS!

RIGHT LEG, LEFT LEG,

ISN'T THIS FUN!

A baby massage rhyme, these words are spoken while an adult holds baby's legs and massages them one at a time. Right hand alternates with the left hand, moving quickly and gently from the thigh downward and off the foot. Tickle baby inside his thigh at end of the poem.

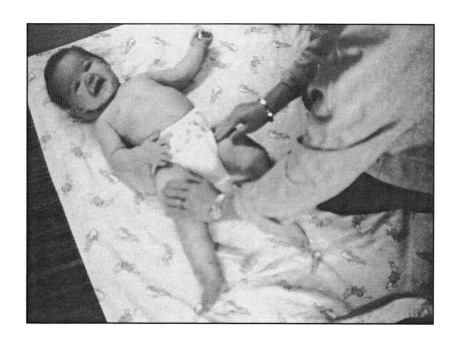

ON MY TRIP TO THE MOUNTAINS

      /   /   /

1. <u>Tap, tap tap</u>, goes the bird in the tree.

      /   /   /

   <u>Tap, tap, tap</u>, goes the bird in the tree.

      /   /   /

   <u>Tap, tap, tap</u>, goes the bird in the tree,

   On my trip to the mountains with **you**.

2. Quack,   quack,   quack,   goes the duck on the pond.

   >>>>>> <<<<<<   >>>>>>

   Quack,   quack,   quack,   goes the duck on the pond.

   >>>>>> <<<<<<   >>>>>>

   Quack,   quack,   quack,   goes the duck on the pond,

   >>>>>> <<<<<<   >>>>>>

   On my trip to the mountains with **you**.

      \   /   \

3. Flip, flip, flop, goes the fish in the water.

      \   /   \

   Flip, flip, flop, goes the fish in the water.

      \   /   \

   Flip, flip, flop, goes the fish in the water,

   And I'll *catch* that fish for **you**!

TONE BLOCK ACTIVITIES:

1. Using the mallet, tap three times on the ribbed tone block, for lines 1-3. At the end of line 4, children carefully point to the teacher or to a friend with the mallet, emphasizing the word "you." Teacher points to someone, too.

2. Scrape three times on the ribbed tone block, using the stick part of the mallet and pressing against the ribs to make a good sound. Emphasize the word "you."

3. Hold the tone block so that the open end becomes a receptacle for the mallet. Place the mallet inside and let go, so that it can gently move right and left to create wooden sounds. On the word "catch," grasp the mallet and remove it from the tone block in time to carefully point it to "you."

Traditional
Lyrics by JANE BROWNE

OWL SONG/WHO ARE YOU?

There's a wise old OWL with a poin-ted NOSE,

two poin-ted EARS and claws for its TOES. It sits in a TREE and it

looks at YOU, flaps its WINGS and it says, "Who, who."

THE OWL SONG By Jane Brown © 1991 Jane Brown / Crown Publishers
All Rights Reserved   Used with Kind Permission

TEACHER SAYS: "Sometimes the owl sings  sometimes

and sometimes MI  When it's your turn you choose."

GESTURES:

OWL: Make pretend eyeglasses with thumb and index fingers of both hands
NOSE: index finger draws the length of your nose
EARS: pinch the top of your ears, pulling up slightly
TOES: point to your toes
TREE: arms make tree shape
YOU: point to someone
WINGS: flap arms

TODDLER, PRE:

Youngest children participate by singing only the emphasized words.

K-PRI:

Kindergarten and primary school age children can sing the song by systematically removing one word and substituting a gesture. OWL is the first word to be replaced with a motion. Repeat the song and leave out OWL and NOSE, and continue until all capitalized words above are replaced with a motion. The last time, perform the entire song with motions, singing only on the "Who, who."

Further elaboration of the song is explained above with solo singing options. The teacher explains and demonstrates the owl singing SO, MI sometimes, MI, DO sometimes, and MI sometimes. Teacher tells child, "if it's your turn, you choose."

Adults can join the "owl choir" as a special ending to this song when they are participating in the music lesson. Everyone chooses which melodic pattern to sing.

OWL SONG/WHO ARE YOU?

TEACHER: SOLO:

Who,   who,   who   are   you?   Tom - my.

This additional solo singing game can be added to the "Owl Song" or sung separately. An owl puppet is the perfect prop to encourage a young child to sing his name. This is a great game for learning new students' names.

PEEK-A-BOO

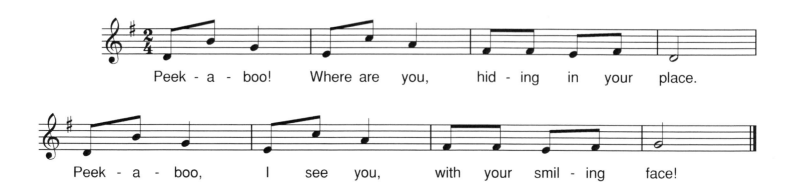

Peek - a - boo! Where are you, hid - ing in your place.

Peek - a - boo, I see you, with your smil - ing face!

Play with a soft, silky scarf while singing this song and hide either baby's face or your own face.

LYNN KLEINER

PERCUSSION FAMILY

1. Here are some wood sounds, wood sounds, wood sounds,
   Lai, lai, lai, lai, lai, lai, lai, lai,
2.-5. *See additional lyrics*

Here are some wood sounds, let me hear them play.
lai, lai, lai, lai, lai, lai, lai, lai, lai.

2. Here are some metal sounds, metal sounds, metal sounds.
   Here are some metal sounds, let me hear them play.
   Lai, lai, lai, lai, lai . . .
3. Here are some shaker sounds . . .
   Lai, lai, lai, lai, lai . . .
4. Here are some skin sounds . . .
   Lai, lai, lai, lai, lai . . .
5. Here are the instruments, instruments, instruments.
   Here are the instruments, percussion family.
   Lai, lai, lai, lai, lai . . .

INSTRUMENTS:

Children sing the lyrics, then improvise on their instruments when the melody is sung again on "lai, lai. . ." Use the pretend microphone during the improvisation to capture some special instrumental solos.

PILGRIM, PILGRIM

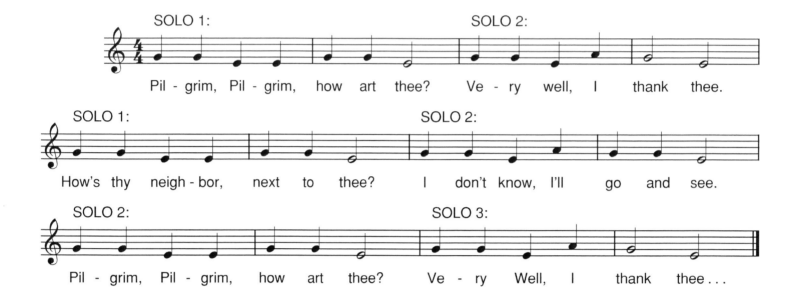

SOLO 1:   SOLO 2:

Pil - grim, Pil - grim, how art thee?   Ve - ry well, I thank thee.

SOLO 1:   SOLO 2:

How's thy neigh-bor, next to thee?   I don't know, I'll go and see.

SOLO 2:   SOLO 3:

Pil - grim, Pil - grim, how art thee?   Ve - ry Well, I thank thee . . .

Children sit in a circle as the solo singing question part is "passed around."
SOLO 1 asks the question.
SOLO 2 answers.
SOLO 1 asks, "How's thy neighbor next to thee?"
SOLO 2 sings, "I don't know, I'll go and see."
The neighbor (SOLO 3) is now brought into the song.

Allow time for children to improvise little singing conversations
with a "pilgrim friend" after everyone in the circle has had a turn.

For Pilgrim finger puppet instructions, see page 103.

POSSUM SONG

Ma - ma and her ba - by went out for a walk one night.

Ma - ma looked be - hind, and babe was gone. What a ter - ri - ble sight!

SOLO MOTHER: SOLO BABY: MOTHER: BABY:

Ba - by!   Ma - ma!   Come back now!   O   K·

This song is performed with a pair of stuffed animal possum puppets— a mother and a baby. As everyone sings, the teacher quickly gives the baby possum to a child to hide. Mama sings first, answered by the child with the possum baby. Mother possum and baby can continue their singing, and improvise a different conversation, or simply follow the lyrics.

When the baby possum is returned to the mother, the game resumes with new solo singers selected by the teacher.

Remind the children that the baby possum tries very hard to match the Mama's tune.

A simple bordun can accompany the "Possum Song."

Words and Music by CARMINO RAVOSA
Arranged by ROSEMARY JACQUES

RED HEN'S SONG

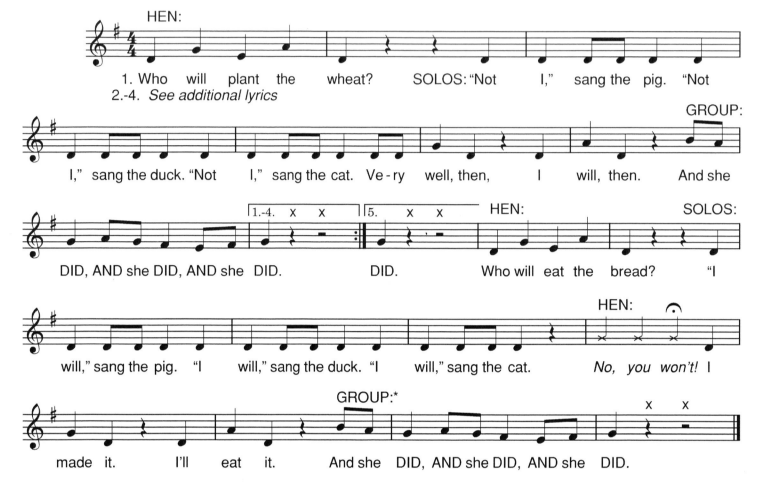

2. Who will cut the wheat?
3. Who'll go to the mill?
4. Who will make the bread?

The performance of this mini-drama is best accomplished with puppets.* You can make the red hen puppet out of a paper bag; the other animals: (pig, duck, and cat,) can be finger puppets.

The phrase "and she did . . ." can be introduced with knee pats/patschen for emphasis. While singing, show the children how to pat these capitalized words:
DID, AND she DID, AND she DID, add two claps at the end.

RED HEN'S SONG

INSTRUMENTS:
Hand drums play on the capitalized words. Tone blocks play on the patterns of two quarter note rests, indicated with Xs in the music. Transfer knee pats to the hand drums, and claps to the tone blocks.

*See pages 102 and 103 for puppet making instructions.

RIDING ON A PONY

Rid - ing on a po - ny, a po - ny, a po - ny.

Rid - ing on a po - ny, here we go. Rid - ing on a po - ny, a

SPOKEN:

po - ny, a po - ny. Rid - ing on a po - ny, *WHOA! WHOA! WHOA!*

Hold baby or toddler securely around ribs. Have baby face outward if there are other children to look at, or face you, if you are alone. Lightly bounce baby on your knees and keep a gentle pulse while singing. On the repeat, stop the bouncing so your child can anticipate this new part:

1st "Whoa!": a slow lean to one side. Then bring back to center and pause.
2nd "Whoa!": a slow lean to the other side. Then bring back to center and pause.
3rd "Whoa!": lift up (and forward, toward others, if child is facing outward), or let the baby slowly lean back if you are facing the baby.

RIG-A-JIG-JIG

As I was walk - ing down the street, down the street,

down the street, a fine mu - si - cian I chanced to meet, hi ho, hi ho, hi ho!

repeat as needed

(Solo 1)   (Solo 2)
Rig - a - jig - jig   Rig - a - jig - jig, LAST TIME: oh . . .

Rig - a - jig - jig and a - way we go, a - way we go, a - way we go.

Rig - a - jig - jig and a - way we go, hi ho, hi ho, hi ho! _____

INSTRUMENTS:

Place small percussion instruments, including shaker eggs, claves, hand drums, and others, on a table.

Solo singers are added one by one in this song; they are chosen by the teacher, who walks around the outside of the circle where the children are sitting. After singing "hi ho . . ." the teacher stops to collect another musician, who chooses an instrument. The teacher sings the "Rig-a-jig-jig" solo (sung on repeated Gs), followed by each chosen musician, down the line. All of the soloists sing the word "Oh," and then skip around the circle.

If you have a large class, the procession can multiply this way: each person in the solo line picks a new child from the circle.

Traditional
Arranged by LYNN KLEINER

ROCK-A-BYE, BABY

Rock-a-bye, ba-by, thy cra-dle is green, Fath-er's a no-ble-man, moth-er's a Queen, and

Bet-ty's a la-dy and wears a gold ring, and John-ny's a drum-mer and drums for the King.

BABY:

Parents gently rock baby or toddler while singing this lullaby.

PRE, K-PRI:

Use this song to explore the gentle playing of chimes, finger cymbals, and triangles. Ask the children to play when they think a beautiful sound should be added to the song. You can tell them to be soft and gentle, and imagine that they are playing for a sleepy baby.

Chords for guitar or piano accompaniment are suggested above.

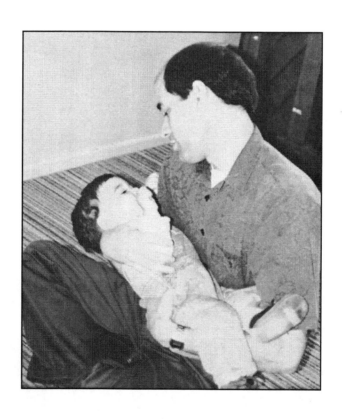

ROLY POLY

POEM	ACTIONS
	Baby is lying on his back.
ROLY POLY, ROLY POLY,	Grasp baby's wrists and keep the beat by making gentle round motions for four counts.
UP, UP, UP.	Move baby's arms up for three counts, and pause.
ROLY POLY, ROLY POLY,	Return to gentle round motions for four counts.
DOWN, DOWN, DOWN.	Move baby's arms down for three counts, and pause.
ROLY POLY, ROLY POLY,	Same as above.
OUT, OUT, OUT.	Move baby's arms outward from the center for three counts, and pause.
ROLY POLY, ROLY POLY,	Same as above.
IN, IN, IN.	Move baby's arms inward for three counts and tickle!

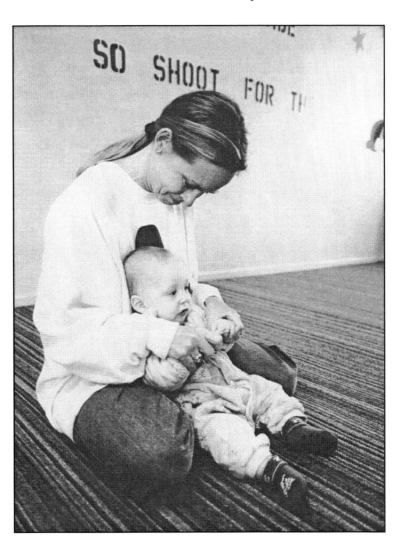

ROUND AND ROUND THE GARDEN

POEM

ROUND AND ROUND THE GARDEN,

LIKE A TEDDY BEAR,

ONE STEP, TWO STEPS,

TICKLE YOU UNDER THERE!

ACTIONS

Hold baby's open hand* and
with your free hand make circular
motions on baby's palm with
your index finger.

With two fingers, rhythmically "walk" up
baby's arm.

Tickle under baby's arm.

*Another way to massage baby during this rhyme is to draw circles on baby's chest and tummy with both hands. "Walk" your fingers up baby's chest. Tickle under baby's chin.

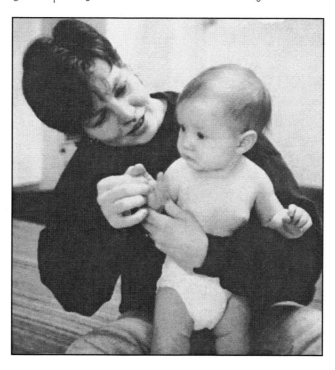

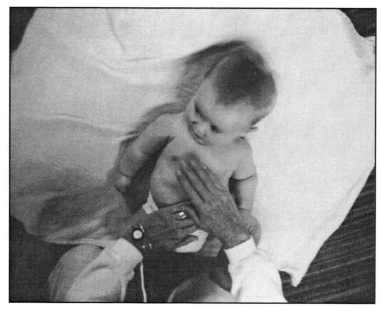

RUM TUM

RUM TUM, RUM TUM,

BABY IS PLAYING ON THE DRUM.

RUM TUM, RUM TUM,

BABY IS PLAYING ON THE DRUM.

BABY:
Sit on the floor with baby sitting in front of you and facing away.
Position your legs on either side of the baby. A hand drum should be
on the floor close to baby, where both of you can reach it. Place
baby's hands on the drum, help him tap the beat, or keep the beat
by tapping it gently with both hands on his back. Make steady
beat sounds on the drum, too, as you speak this poem rhythmically.
Insert baby's name.

TODDLER, PRE, K:
Children can suggest different ways to play the drum, inserting new words on lines two and four.
Suggestions may include:
      "Making wind sounds on my drum."
      "Dancing fingers on my drum."
      "Two hands are playing on my drum."

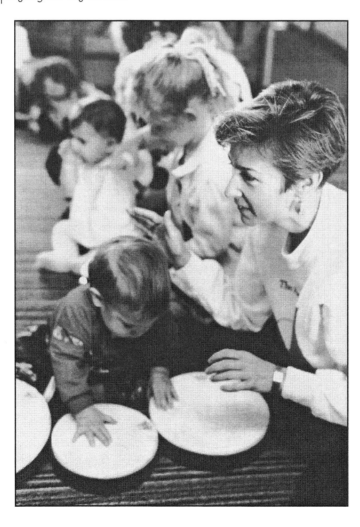

SHAKE AND STOP

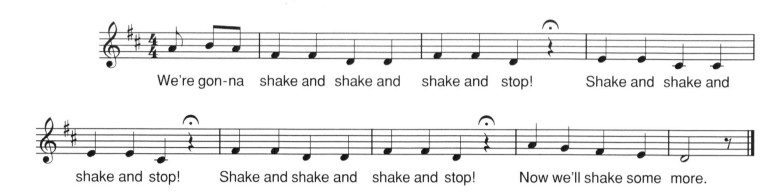

We're gon-na shake and shake and shake and stop! Shake and shake and

shake and stop! Shake and shake and shake and stop! Now we'll shake some more.

BABIES AND TODDLERS:

The teacher should sing and play the song once while holding several maracas, rather than passing out the instruments first. While singing a second time, the teacher can hand a maraca to one child at a time, releasing the instrument exactly on the word, "Stop!"

PRE, K-PRI:

Ask the children to think of an interesting statue pose to hold during each of the silences. There can be a leader whom everyone copies.

SHAKE THOSE BELLS

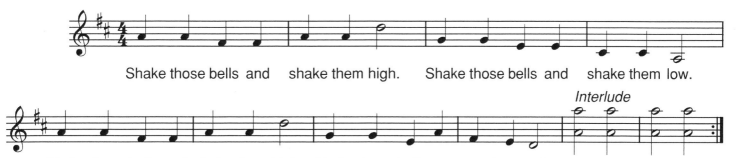

Shake those bells and   shake them high.   Shake those bells and   shake them low.

Interlude

Shake those bells and shake them high. Shake those bells, a - round you go!

INSTRUMENTS:

Children shake the bells high or low, depending on the lyrics. Let them decide where to freeze-hold the bells for the four counts of the interlude. Older children like to think of four different places to freeze-hold the bells on each interlude. Play the interlude on a glockenspiel or keep the rhythm on a hand drum or other similar instrument.

SHOE A LITTLE HORSE

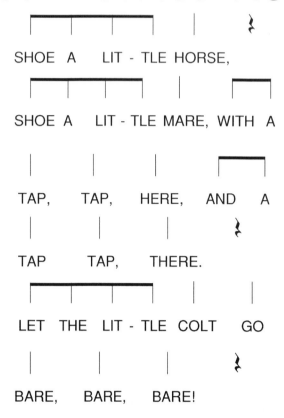

SHOE A   LIT - TLE HORSE,

SHOE A   LIT - TLE MARE, WITH A

TAP,   TAP,   HERE,   AND   A

TAP   TAP,   THERE.

LET THE LIT - TLE COLT   GO

BARE,   BARE,   BARE!

BABY:

With baby on his back, grasp baby's ankles and tap them together to keep the beat as you speak this rhyme. Tickle baby's feet lightly on each "BARE, BARE, BARE!"

TODDLER:

You can tap the beat gently on your child's shoulders, or gently bounce him on your knees while the rhyme is recited. Repeat the rhyme at different tempos.

PRE:

Older children enjoy this rhyme, too. They can play rhythm sticks or tone blocks while the rhyme is recited each time at different tempos. You can tap the beat gently on your child's shoulders to reinforce the different tempos.

K-PRI:

As with dozens of nursery rhymes, a simple bordun can accompany "Shoe a Little Horse."

A pentatonic melody can be improvised, replicating the rhythm of the words. The higher pitched instruments, including the glockenspiels, can then be played on the rests. Any of the notes in C pentatonic may be selected for these sound clusters.

C PENTATONIC BARS

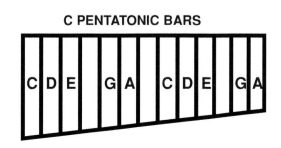

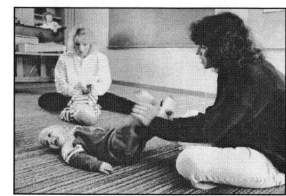

SILLY SAM

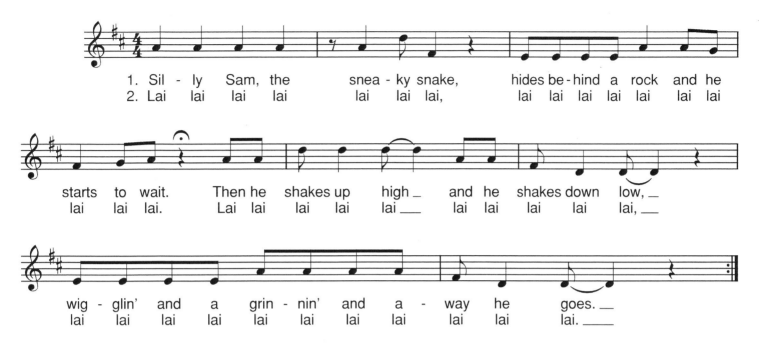

1. Sil - ly Sam, the snea - ky snake, hides be - hind a rock and he
2. Lai lai lai lai lai lai lai, lai lai lai lai lai lai lai

starts to wait. Then he shakes up high _ and he shakes down low, _
lai lai lai. Lai lai lai lai lai ___ lai lai lai lai lai, ___

wig - glin' and a grin - nin' and a - way he goes. _
lai lai lai lai lai lai lai lai lai lai lai. ___

The instrument for "Silly Sam" is a shaker egg. Cued by the lyrics and following the teacher's example, children hold their shakers behind them when Sam (the puppet) hides behind a rock. After the "wait," which can last as long as the teacher desires, the children bring out their eggs and shake them high and low, until the end of the song.

For verse 2, the teacher gives the snake puppet to a child, who becomes "Silly Sam." This person leads the song and decides how long to hide behind the rock.

The snake is easily made out of a sock. From inside the sock, your hand can grasp the shaker egg.

SIMONE AND OTTO

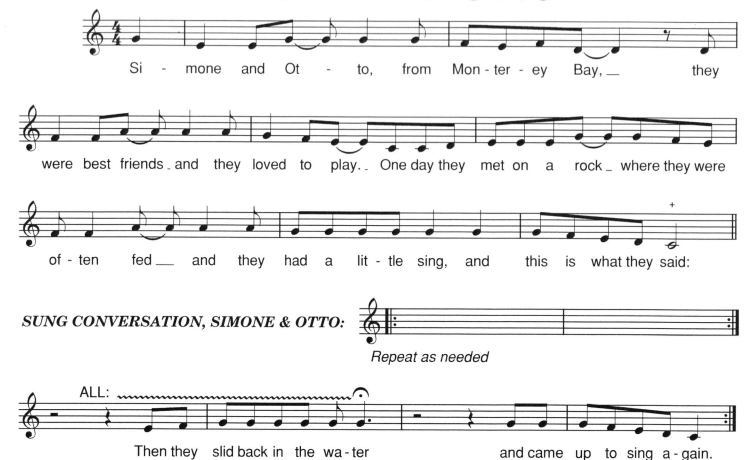

Si - mone and Ot - to, from Mon - ter - ey Bay, ___ they

were best friends _ and they loved to play. _ One day they met on a rock _ where they were

of - ten fed ___ and they had a lit - tle sing, and this is what they said:

SUNG CONVERSATION, SIMONE & OTTO:

Repeat as needed

ALL:

Then they slid back in the wa - ter and came up to sing a - gain.

Children stand in a circle with a shaker egg in hand. Two soloists sit in the middle of the circle on chairs which represent the rocks.

The soloists hold their puppets; Simone the Seal and Otto the Otter. Everyone sings the song and dances with shaker eggs.

After "this is what they said," the children put their eggs on the floor and listen quietly to the singing dialogue between Simone and Otto. The children know when the singing is over because the soloists sing goodbye to each other. While singing, "Then they slide back in the water," the children make a tremolo by patting rapidly on their legs. Simone and Otto leave the rocks (the chairs) and pretend to slide into the water; they come up to give the puppets to new solo singers.

Traditional
Arranged by LYNN KLEINER

SOMEBODY'S KNOCKIN'

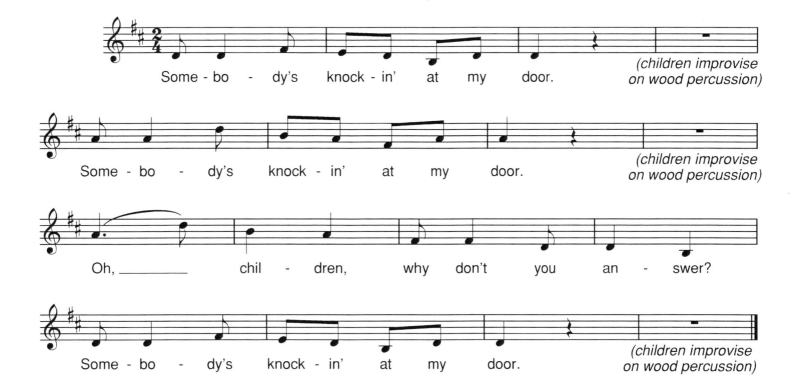

Some - bo - dy's knock - in' at my door.   *(children improvise on wood percussion)*

Some - bo - dy's knock - in' at my door.   *(children improvise on wood percussion)*

Oh, _____ chil - dren, why don't you an - swer?

Some - bo - dy's knock - in' at my door.   *(children improvise on wood percussion)*

TODDLER, PRE:

Each child holds a mallet (or a rhythm stick). The teacher moves from child to child, holding out the tone block or rhythm stick just at the right time for the child to improvise. Teacher keeps moving to surprise and select a different child for each solo part. After the children know when to play, let them play with a complete instrument: tone block and mallet, or two rhythm sticks.

K-PRI:

Children have ribbed tone blocks and mallets. Teacher asks each child to show a way to produce knocking patterns, then selects one of these ways for everyone to try with the song. Rhythm sticks can also be employed.

STARS

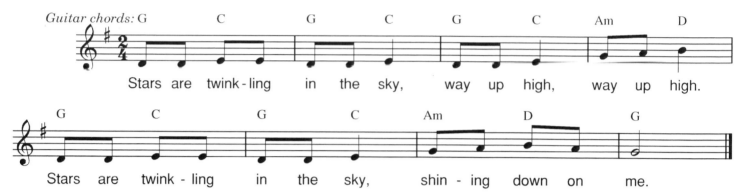

Stars are twink - ling in the sky, way up high, way up high.

Stars are twink - ling in the sky, shin - ing down on me.

STAR LIGHT

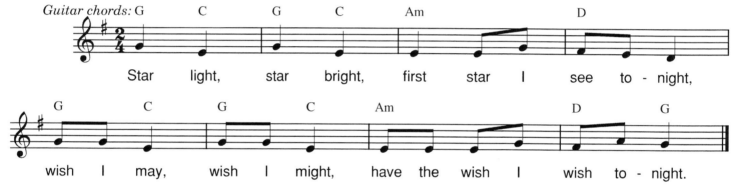

Star light, star bright, first star I see to - night,

wish I may, wish I might, have the wish I wish to - night.

BABY:

During these songs, babies enjoy holding one finger cymbal which is struck by an adult who holds the matching finger cymbal. Babies also love to touch their finger cymbal to the hanging chimes, or to watch an adult play the chimes for them.

TODDLER, PRE, K-PRI:

Invite the children to play the triangle or finger cymbals whenever they think it would sound best.

Traditional Melody
Arranged by LYNN KLEINER

STORMY DAY

1. The rain on the win-dow goes tap, tap, tap, tap, tap, tap,
2.-5. *See additional lyrics*

tap, tap, tap. The rain on the win-dow goes tap, tap, tap, on a storm-y day.

2. The wipers on the cars go swish, swish, swish . . . on a stormy day.
3. The wind in the trees go whoo, whoo, whoo . . . on a stormy day.
4. The hail on the roof goes thump, thump, thump . . . on a stormy day.
5. The thunder in the clouds goes boom, boom, boom . . . on a stormy day.

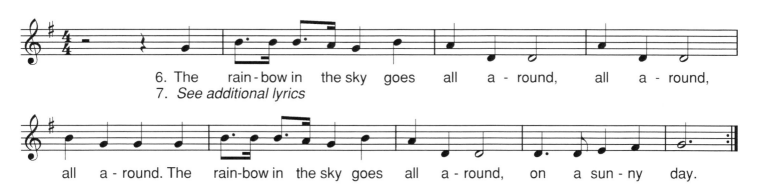

6. The rain-bow in the sky goes all a - round, all a - round,
7. *See additional lyrics*

all a - round. The rain-bow in the sky goes all a - round, on a sun - ny day.

7. The children in the park all dance and play . . . on a sunny day.

Children are sitting on the floor with a hand drum directly in front of them. Give each child a scarf to hide underneath the hand drum. Keeping the drum on the floor, children play the drum head as suggested in the lyrics for verses one through five.

While singing verse six, the children retrieve the scarf and use the color and movement to suggest a rainbow. On verse seven, the children stand up with the drum and the scarf to dance and play about the room for the conclusion to "A Stormy Day."

Teacher can point out that the storm (g minor) contrasts with the sound of the rainbow (G major).

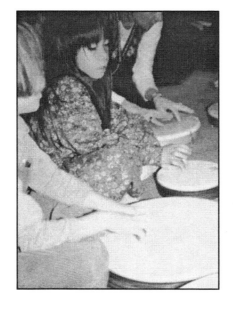

THIS IS THE WAY THE LADIES RIDE

POEM	ACTIONS
THIS IS THE WAY THE LADIES RIDE,	Speak rhythmically in a high voice. Keep the beat by bouncing baby gently on your knees.
PRIM, PRIM, PRIM, PRIM!	
THIS IS THE WAY THE GENTLEMEN RIDE,	Speak in a low voice. Bounce a little higher.
TRIM, TRIM, TRIM, TRIM!	
THIS IS THE WAY THE HUNTERS RIDE,	Use a "hunter" voice and increase the bouncing tempo a little.
A-GALLOP, A-GALLOP, A-GALLOP, A-GALLOP.	
THIS IS THE WAY THE FARMERS RIDE,	Speak in lower voice.
HOBBLETY HO, HOBBLETY HO,	Move baby from side-to-side. Rock on the beat, instead of bouncing.
HOBBLETY, HOBBLETY, HOBBLETY HO!	

In this chair/lap game babies and toddlers should face outward, if in a group. Otherwise, they should face the adult.

THIS IS THE WAY WE PLAY

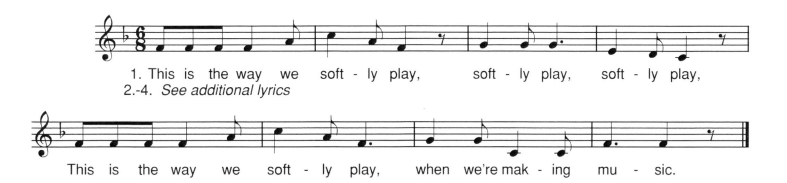

1. This is the way we soft - ly play, soft - ly play, soft - ly play,
2.-4. *See additional lyrics*

This is the way we soft - ly play, when we're mak - ing mu - sic.

2. This is the way we loudly play
3. This is the way we slowly play
4. This is the way we quickly play

INSTRUMENTS:

Words cue the children's playing on a variety of percussion instruments. The tambourine and hand drum are good choices for loud vs. soft and fast vs. slow. Be sure to try the song SLOW and LOUD simultaneously, as well as FAST and SOFT. Pausing between verses is a good idea; it helps the children to focus.

TRANSITION SONGS

Each of these songs was created to help the teacher initiate new activities in smooth sequence. While singing, the children will know whether to move into a new formation, pick up new instruments, or put their instruments away.

PRE, K-PRI

Adapted by LYNN KLEINER

LETS MAKE A CIRCLE

Let's make a cir - cle, a great big cir - cle.

Let's make a cir - cle and a - way we go.

Other useful lyrics are:

Let's make a circle and we'll all hold hands.
Let's make a circle and we'll all sit down.

Repeat "let's make a circle and away we go" until the group is ready to sit down (end with these words, "all sit down").

Adapted by LYNN KLEINER

GENTLY BACK

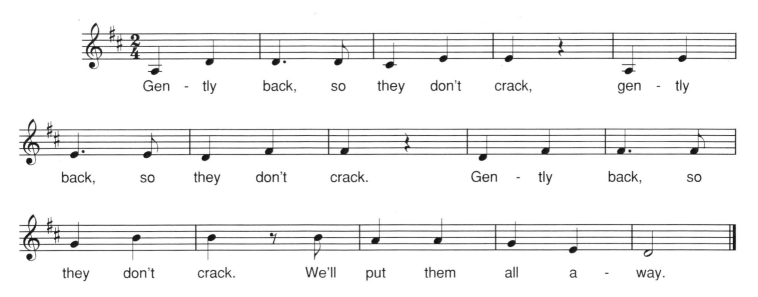

Gen - tly back, so they don't crack, gen - tly back, so they don't crack. Gen - tly back, so they don't crack. We'll put them all a - way.

Other useful lyrics are:

Strikers high, as I come by.
Mallets high, as I come by.

Also, before collecting instruments, the teacher can initiate a listening game, telling the children, for example, to "put your striker on the floor, put your striker on your knee . . . on your shoulder . . . head . . . up high . . . higher . . . way up high." This leads into the song, "Strikers (or mallets) High, As I Come By."

Adapted by LYNN KLEINER

DRUMS AWAY

Drums* a - way,   drums a - way,   that is   all   for   them to - day.

*triangles, wood blocks, finger cymbals, etc.

Triangles, wood blocks, finger cymbals, and so on, may be substituted for drums in this song. If drums are the instrument, the teacher can start the song with a strong beat, and direct the children to march as they sing. One by one the children form a line to return their instrument to the container.

Each of these songs promotes care and respect for the instruments.

TWO LITTLE EYES

POEM	ACTIONS
TWO LITTLE EYES TO LOOK AROUND.	Massage baby's forehead and move fingers around his eyes.
TWO LITTLE EARS TO HEAR EACH SOUND.	Now move fingers to the backs of the ears and under the chin.
ONE LITTLE NOSE TO SMELL WHAT'S SWEET.	Now move from the forehead to the tip of the nose.
AND ONE LITTLE MOUTH THAT LIKES TO EAT.	Draw a smile with your index fingers first above, then below the baby's lips.

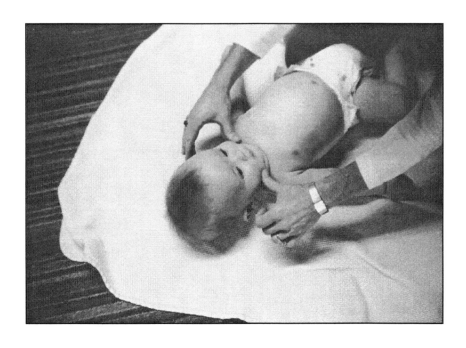

This massage rhyme can be spoken to a baby, who is lying on his back, or to a toddler, who is facing an adult, at eye level.

Traditional
Arranged by LYNN KLEINER

TWO LITTLE SAUSAGES

POEM	INSTRUMENT SOUNDS
BREAKFAST!	*Say this word slowly as if a triangle were ringing to call everyone to the table.*
TWO LITTLE SAUSAGES	*maracas*
FRYING IN A PAN.	*maracas*
ONE GOES "POP!"	*rhythm sticks*
AND THE OTHER GOES "BAM!"	*tambourine or drum*

Children enjoy trying to play all four instruments to accompany this rhyme; a slow tempo will help them. Children are seated on the floor with their set of instruments in front of them.

For variation, assign each instrument to a different child to play.

Still another idea is to just use hands and legs to imitate cooking sounds. Rub hands for the frying sausages. Clap cupped hands for the "pop," and pat legs once (or stamp on the floor) to emphasize "bam!"

LYNN KLEINER

UP SO HIGH

Up so high,   down so low.   Give a lit - tle shake and a - round we go.

Up so high,   down so low.   Give a lit - tle shake, now   hold them so.

Like the song, "Shake and Stop," "Up So High" gives children an opportunity to move in place as they sing and shake their maracas.

TODDLER:
Follow the teacher's movements and "freeze-hold" at the end.

PRE, K-PRI:
One child can lead the others, choosing a "freeze-hold" for all to copy at "hold them so."

A VERY HILLY PLACE - Story Song

Puppets can be used for the characters, or children can use simple props with special movements to show the personality of their chosen characters.

VERSE	CHARACTERS	INSTRUMENTS
1	THE BOY (OR GIRL)	hand drum
2	THE FROG	guiro or ribbed wooden tone block
3	THE SNAKE	shaker egg or maraca
4	THE BIRD	finger cymbals
5	TRAIN	additional hand drum, train whistle
6	ALL	all instruments

As shown in verse 1, the song's accompaniment will always consist of a bordun and a glissando. The glissando is to be played on the words "up" and "down." Also, two measures of the bordun will provide an introduction to the melody each time it is sung.

One child, who is the BOY, pretends to be leading a parade as he sings the song and plays his drum on the rests. (Other children can join the BOY to play the drum part. The children can play in groups or can play individually on the other instrumental parts.)

TEACHER:

Once upon a time there was a boy who lived in a very hilly part of the country. One day, the boy took his drum and went out for a walk. He said, "I wish I had a band to follow me." He sang:

(One child who is the BOY pretends to be leading a parade.)

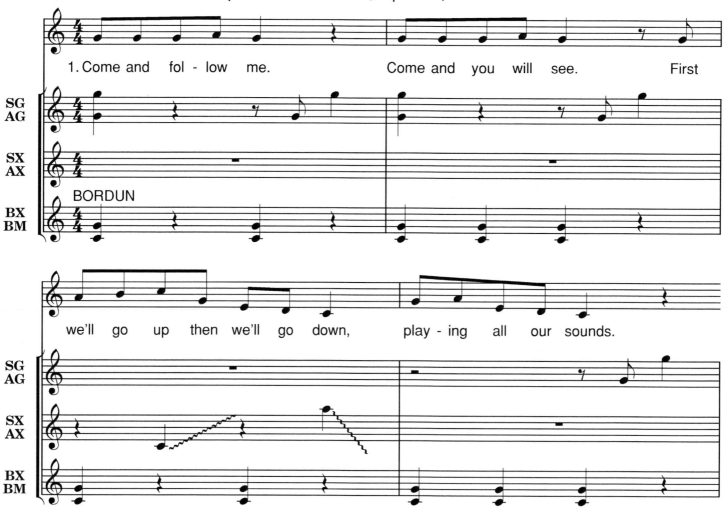

ALL: He went up, up, up, up, up, the hill
and down, down, down, down, down the hill.

A VERY HILLY PLACE - Story Song

TEACHER: And when he got to the bottom, he stopped to take a rest.
At first he did not notice, but then he listened carefully and heard . . .

(FROG or FROG GROUP plays a scraping sound on a ribbed tone block or guiro.)

He looked around and saw a frog sitting next to a tree.

(Play ribbed tone block/guiro again.)

The boy invited the frog to follow him.

BOY: "Would you like to follow me?"

FROG: "Sure!"

(Begin song again, with guiro and drum playing on the rests. Boy and Frog move in the parade.)

2. Come and fol - low me. Come and you will see. First

we'll go up, then we'll go down, play - ing all our sounds.

ALL: They went up, up, up, up, up the hill
and down, down, down, down, down the hill.

TEACHER: And when they got to the bottom, they stopped to take a rest. At first they did not
notice, but then they listened carefully and heard . . .

(SNAKE or SNAKE GROUP plays shaker egg.)

They looked around, and saw something coiled around the tree. It was a snake.

(Shaker sound again.)

They invited the snake to follow them.

BOY AND FROG: "Would you like to follow us?"

SNAKE: "Sure!"

**(Begin song again with hand drum, guiro, and shaker playing on rests. Boy, frog, and snake
move in parade.)**

A VERY HILLY PLACE - Story Song

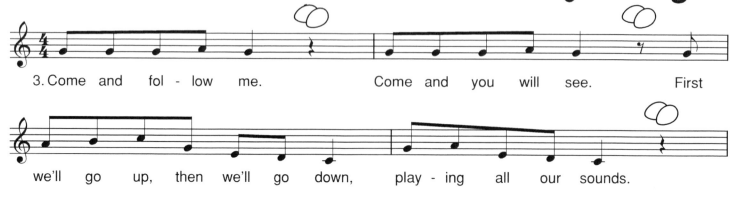

3. Come and fol - low me. Come and you will see. First

we'll go up, then we'll go down, play - ing all our sounds.

ALL: They went up, up, up, up, up the hill,
and down, down, down, down, down the hill.

TEACHER: And when they got to the bottom, they stopped to take a rest. At first they did not notice, but then they listened carefully and heard. . .

(BIRD or BIRD GROUP plays finger cymbals.)

They looked around, and saw, sitting in the tree, a bird. They invited the bird to follow them.

BOY, FROG, SNAKE: "Would you like to follow us?"

BIRD: "Sure!"

(Begin song again with finger cymbals, drum, guiro, and shaker. Boy, frog, snake, and bird move in parade.)

4. Come and fol - low me. Come and you will see. First

we'll go up, then we'll go down, play - ing all our sounds.

ALL: They went up, up, up, up, up the hill,
and down, down, down, down, down the hill.

TEACHER: And when they got to the bottom, they stopped to take a rest.
They were so very tired. The boy asked the frog:

BOY: "Are you ready to go home?"

FROG: "No, I'm too tired."

TEACHER: The frog asked the snake:

FROG: "Are you ready to go home?"

SNAKE: "No, I'm too tired."

TEACHER: The snake asked the bird:

SNAKE: "Are you ready?"

A VERY HILLY PLACE - Story Song

BIRD: "I'm too tired."

TEACHER: At first they did not notice, but then they listened carefully and they heard:

(Child plays hand drum, using circular motions on the drum head to make the sound of the train.)

It was the little train.

ALL CHILDREN: "Will you give us a ride back to our homes?"

TRAIN: "Sure!"

(All instruments play on rests now.)

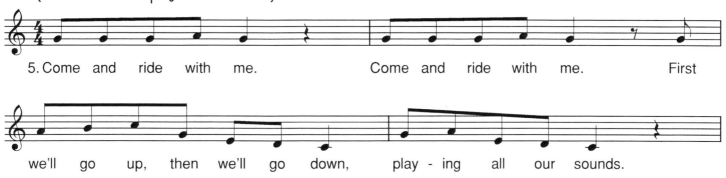

5. Come and ride with me. Come and ride with me. First
we'll go up, then we'll go down, play - ing all our sounds.

TEACHER: So they climbed aboard, and the train went
up, up, up, up, up (soloist plays the drum slowly) and
down, down, down, down, down (soloist plays the drum fast), down every hill, 'til they were all home.
I wonder who will follow the boy next time he sings . . .

(All sing. All instruments play on rests.)

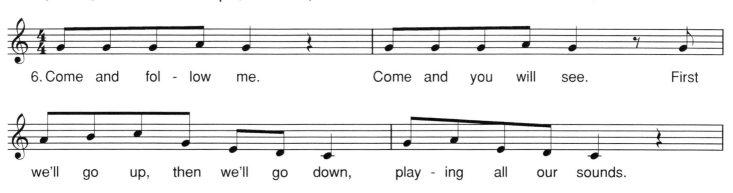

6. Come and fol - low me. Come and you will see. First
we'll go up, then we'll go down, play - ing all our sounds.

WALTER, WALTER WAGTAIL

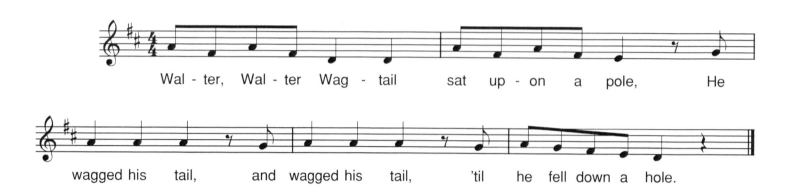

Wal - ter, Wal - ter Wag - tail   sat   up - on   a   pole,   He

wagged his   tail,   and wagged his   tail,   'til he fell down a hole.

Babies and toddlers enjoy this chair/lap game. Facing outward and held securely, they are gently bounced to the beat of the song. At "he wagged his tail . . ." adults switch their leg motion from up and down, to side to side. (It helps to keep your heels off the floor when you move your knees in parallel motion from side to side.) Maintain the beat with your motions until the end. Then lift the baby or toddler, and place him on the floor while still holding the child. Pause, and bring him back up to your lap to sing the song all over again.

WASH THE DISHES

POEM	ACTIONS
WASH THE DISHES, WASH THE DISHES,	Massage baby's chest with downward strokes keeping the beat as indicated.
RING THE BELL FOR TEA.	On "tea," gently touch baby's nose.
THREE GOOD WISHES, THREE GOOD KISSES,	Massage chest again.
I WILL GIVE TO THEE.	On "thee," gently touch baby's nose.
ONE . . .	Give a kiss on one cheek.
TWO . . .	Give a kiss on the other cheek.
THREE! . . .	Give kisses all over!

Baby, in diaper, lies on his back on a blanket. Using a natural baby oil enhances this wonderful massage rhyme.

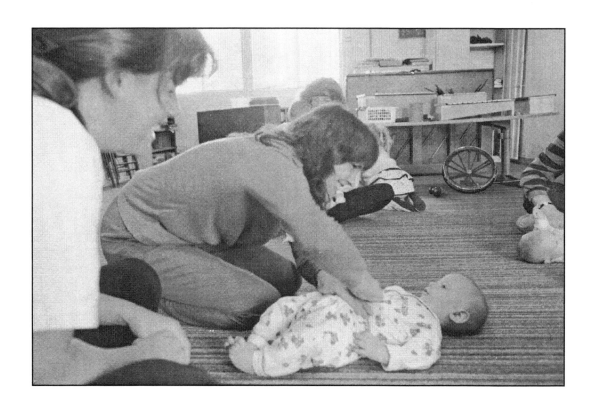

WHEN SHEEP GET UP IN THE MORNING

ALL:

1. When *sheep get up in the morn - ing they say, "Good day! Good

day!" When sheep get up in the morn - ing they say, "Good day! Good

SOLO: **ALL:**

day!" They say "Baa, baa, baa, baa." And this is what they

SOLO:

say, they say. "Baa, baa, baa, baa" and this is what they say.

A simple bordun can accompany "When Sheep Get Up in the Morning."

The solo section can also be sung on different pitches (rather than with animal sounds on the SO-MI pattern); these selected pitches can be performed as an echo with the teacher, or as an improvisation.

Children enjoy selecting other animals such as dogs, cats, and so on, and their ways to sing "Good morning!" The animal sounds can accumulate, providing further musical challenges.

Traditional
Arranged by LYNN KLEINER

WHO'S THAT?

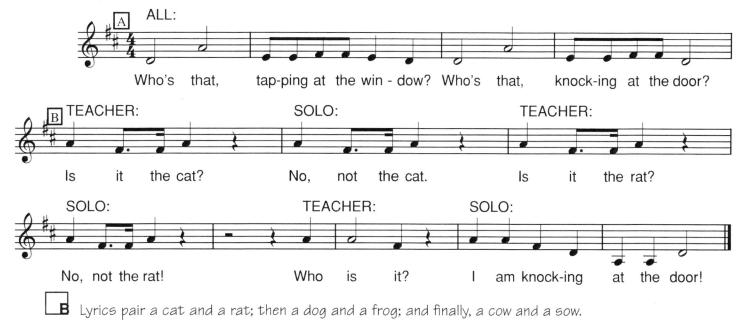

A ALL:

Who's that, tap-ping at the win-dow? Who's that, knock-ing at the door?

B TEACHER: | SOLO: | TEACHER:

Is it the cat? | No, not the cat. | Is it the rat?

SOLO: | TEACHER: | SOLO:

No, not the rat! | Who is it? | I am knock-ing at the door!

 **B** Lyrics pair a cat and a rat; then a dog and a frog; and finally, a cow and a sow.

Children with finger puppets* answer the teacher's questions,
   "Is it the cat?" and so on, continuing with the rest of the puppets: dog, frog, cow, and sow.

PRE:

After playing an improvised knocking rhythm on the ribbed tone block, the solo player is
asked by the teacher,
   "Who is it?" "I am knocking at the door," is the soloist's reply.

K-PRI:

One child hides and sings the solo; the others, with eyes closed, try to guess who it is.

A simple bordun can accompany "Who's That?"

*See page 103 for puppet making instructions.

This song can be paired with "Somebody's Knockin" p. 79.

WIGGLEY WOO

ALL: SOLO:

Come on out now, Wig-gley Woo. (Tom) will sing "Hel - lo" to you.   Hel - lo!

A simple bordun can accompany the song, "Wiggley Woo."

Invite one child to sing the solo, rewarding him by bringing out the worm in the apple puppet.*

*See page 104 for puppet making instructions.

Traditional

YONDER SHE COMES

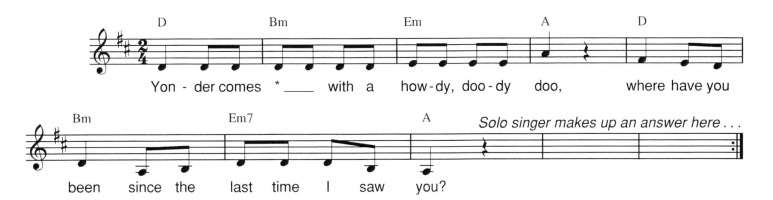

Yon - der comes * ____ with a how - dy, doo - dy doo, where have you been since the last time I saw you?

Solo singer makes up an answer here . . .

The question in this song invites solo singing. Teacher asks who would like his name sung. Group sings the song, and the child whose name is sung sings an answer. The answer can be anything from a true summer vacation story to a made-up tale of a trip to Mars.

PUPPETS

MAKE YOUR OWN SINGING FINGER PUPPET

Cut the fingers off an old glove (such as a cotton gardening glove).
If you have no glove, you can simply draw a face on your finger with a water-based marking pen. You can also stitch two pieces of felt or other dense fabric together in the shape of a finger. Turn the stitched pieces inside out. Draw, stitch or glue the eyes, nose, mouth and other facial traits on the finger puppet.

MAKE YOUR OWN SINGING POP-UP PUPPET

Materials Needed:
- a dowel or chop stick
- a small styrofoam ball for the head
- a 1-pound coffee can
- a colorful sock (to pull over the puppet head and down over the top of the can)
- some felt or a thick fabric to wrap around the outside of the can
- some yarn or other goodies to decorate the puppet
- masking tape, rubber band, pins and fabric glue to hold it all together.

Directions:
1. Remove the top and bottom of your empty can and cover any sharp edges with thick masking or duct tape.

2. Insert the stick into the styrofoam ball to make a hole. Remove it. Use fabric glue and reinforce the stick's end with a tiny scrap of fabric. Glue and push this fabric into the ball.

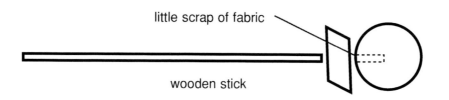

little scrap of fabric

wooden stick

PUPPETS

3. Pull the stretch sock over the styrofoam ball, positioning the toe section over the part that will become the puppet's head. Secure the puppet's head at the neck with a tight rubber band or string.

4. Insert the other end of the dowel into the can. Stretch the rest of the sock over the rim of the can. Tape the bottom edge of the sock to the can after adjusting it so that it will stand on a table without sagging or falling over.

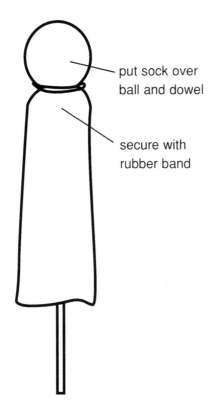

put sock over
ball and dowel

secure with
rubber band

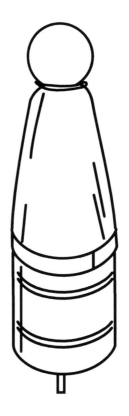

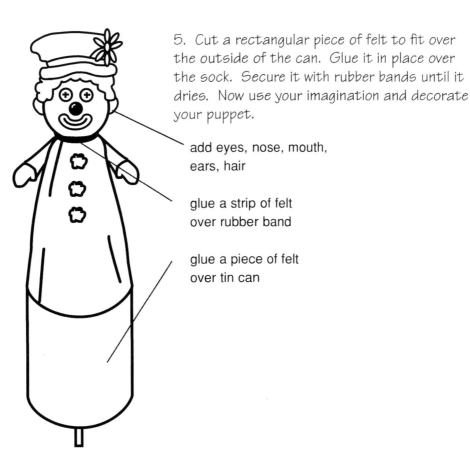

5. Cut a rectangular piece of felt to fit over the outside of the can. Glue it in place over the sock. Secure it with rubber bands until it dries. Now use your imagination and decorate your puppet.

add eyes, nose, mouth,
ears, hair

glue a strip of felt
over rubber band

glue a piece of felt
over tin can

PUPPETS

MAKE YOUR OWN LITTLE RED HEN PAPER BAG PUPPET

1. Start with a brown paper lunch bag. With additional brown construction paper, cut out a circle that is as wide as your lunch bag.

2. Glue the full circle to the bag's bottom (the flap).

3. Cut out two yellow felt (or paper) triangles for the puppet's beak.

4. Glue the beak onto the paper; one part goes on top of the full circle, and the other one is glued underneath. The tips of the beak should extend a bit beyond the circle as shown in the illustration below.

5. Cut scallops around a rectangular piece of red felt or red paper for the hen's comb. Fold and glue the comb on top of the hen's head.

6. Add eyes to your hen with marking pens or scraps of fabric.

Place your hand inside the bag to operate the beak as you sing the "Little Red Hen" song.

PUPPETS

MAKE YOUR OWN PAPER FINGER PUPPETS

for characters in the "Red Hen's Song," "When Sheep Get Up," "Pilgrim Song," and other songs which have singing characters.

Photocopy the following finger puppet illustrations and transfer the drawings onto stiff paper. Cut the patterns out and staple or tape the ends together so the puppets fit like rings on your fingers.

PUPPETS

MAKE YOUR OWN PAPER CUP PUPPET

A styrofoam or paper cup, a popsicle stick, and an illustration from the previous page are all that is needed to create a paper cup puppet.
Cut a slot at the bottom of the cup and slide the popsicle stick through. Glue the illustration to the popsicle stick.

MAKE YOUR OWN WIGGLEY WORM PUPPET

Using the sketch here for the approximate dimensions, stitch together red or green felt to create an apple shape a little larger than the size of your fist. Make one opening for a finger-sized worm. Your index finger will poke out from this opening, disguised as a worm.

INDEX

INDEX

INDEX

INDEX

INDEX

RELATED AUDIO AND VIDEO PRODUCTS

The CD
Kids Make Music, Babies Make Music Too! - CD (#6001)
contains most of the songs, rhymes and dances from this book beautifully orchestrated for Orff tone-bar and percussion instruments.

The VIDEOS
The videos show babies and children making music and feature models of excellent music teaching. The tapes are popular for families at home, day care centers, and schools, and are used for teacher training and as great fund raising items for school music programs!

"Lynn Kleiner's musicianship and fine pedagogy offer a dynamic model for teachers. Lynn is truly a master teacher!"
Lori Custodero, Professor from University of Southern California

BABIES MAKE MUSIC - VIDEO (#1002)
Babies and toddlers instinctively react to music! The variety of activities in this landmark video will stimulate the baby's natural responses, while developing a sense of timing, pitch and aural and language skills. Also included is a guide to teachers and parents by Dr. Donna Brink Fox, a leading authority on Early Childhood Music Education from the Eastman School of Music.

"The first time my baby smiled, it was while we were playing one of the games from BABIES MAKE MUSIC. I know what I'm giving for baby shower gifts! Every infant and new parent should have this video!"
Michelle Dunn, Parent and second grade teacher.

KIDS MAKE MUSIC - VIDEO (#1001)
This wonderful video for toddlers and preschool age children contains songs, rhymes and dances. Children love to coordinate their musicmaking at home or school while watching Lynn and her children in the music room, a park and even a fire station! Following the lessons, Lynn includes suggestions for parents and teachers on vocal and rhythmic development and comments on the benefits of the early musical experience.

"My favorite part is when Lynn drives the fire truck and I play the triangle!"
Daniel Kelleher, 3-year-old musician, Manhattan Beach, CA

KIDS MAKE MUSIC TOO! - VIDEO (#1003)
For ages 2-8, the activities include more specific percussion playing, improvisation, musical concepts and vocabulary. The setting includes the music room, a farm, a park and a ride on a carousel and train.

THE INSTRUMENTS
KIDS MAKE MUSIC - INSTRUMENT KIT (#4001)
tambourine, rhythm sticks, triangle, jingle bells, maraca.

KIDS MAKE MUSIC TOO! - INSTRUMENT KIT (#5003)
REMO hand drum, colorful scarf, shaker egg, guiro tone block, finger cymbals.

For workshop, product information, or to locate a dealer near you call **1-888-TRY-MUSIC** or **310-376-8646.**

KIDS MAKE MUSIC and KIDS MAKE MUSIC TOO! And the instrument kits have become our daughter's favorite activity and number one video choice. It's replaced Barney and Elmo! We love to watch her dance, sing and play the instruments and we've seen how her sense of timing has improved!"
David Liesenfelt, Father of a 2-year-old, Chicago, IL

ABOUT THE AUTHORS

LYNN KLEINER

Lynn Kleiner is founder and director of Music Rhapsody, a music school based in Manhattan Beach, California for parents and infants, toddlers and young children through the 8th grade. She also directs Music Rhapsody's Summer Music Day Camp for children ages 5 - 14. A popular clinician for pre-schools, school districts, Orff-Schulwerk chapters and parent groups, Lynn has also presented sessions at many national conferences for the American Orff-Schulwerk Association and the Music Educators National Conference. Her award-winning videos, "Babies Make Music," "Kids Make Music," and "Kids Make Music Too!" for the early childhood years have been very popular with parents and teachers of young children. Kleiner's Orff-Schulwerk training and her Master's certificate were earned at Memphis State University.

CECILIA RIDDELL

Cecilia Riddell has taught music and music education at California State University, Dominguez Hills since 1972. A graduate of Pomona College and Harvard University Graduate School of Education, she received her Ph.D. in Music from U.C.L.A. A former choral conductor and pianist, she received her Orff Level III certificate from U.S.C. in 1974. Riddell has written many articles and has presented numerous workshops for local, state and national music associations. In addition to teaching at the university level, Riddell offers Saturday classes for babies and parents, and for pre-school children. She was named "Teacher of the Year" in 1994 by the California Music Educators Association, Southern Section.